..... & ELI SUSSMAN

Classic Recipes

for

MODERN PEOPLE

PHOTOGRAPHY
Erin Kunkel

ILLUSTRATION
Jon Contino

OLIVE PRESS

1
CLASSICS
from our
CHILDHOOD

PAGE 13

Our mom and dad were vegetable-loving, always-cooking-from-scratch, no-microwave-owning, cable-TV-shunning, book-loving, snack-food-hating parents. (We're working on our pitch for a wacky-artist-mom, strict-lawyer-dad sitcom right now; it's called *Liberal Justice*.) And while the above may not sound like an ideal culinary childhood if you were into Lunchables and Oreos, we have amazing food memories that we're going to share with you here. As we all can attest, having a terrible or fantastic food childhood can shape your relationship with food for life. Certain things that you eat when you are young can take on mythical elements. We're taking the dishes our family cooked and tweaking them into the modern era.

2
CLASSICS
from your
CHILDHOOD

PAGE 33

By utilizing the World Wide Web, you can travel to new lands, obtain useless info by the truckload, watch super-stupid videos, and discover flavor combos that you've never heard of before. One night, while taking a spin on this information superhighway, we discovered that not everyone grew up white, Jewish, and suburban and therefore might not have the same idea of what defines a classic dish. So we channeled this great modern power known as social media and asked our friends for their favorite childhood dishes. We were overwhelmed with how many personal classics were submitted. And because mostly it was stuff we never ate growing up, we were intrigued to approach it from an outsider's perspective. So brace yourself and travel with us back in time to your childhood, where we're reimagining all the delectable dishes we heard about but never got to eat growing up.

3
TV dinner
CLASSICS

PAGE 49

We can honestly say that we've never eaten a TV dinner in front of a TV in our lives. It's not that we're above that. It's just that our family didn't roll like that (but boy oh boy did that make us want, worse than anything, to eat Swanson while watching *The Simpsons*). And don't knock us for not engaging in a whole lot of eating R&D for this chapter. Eli ate a microwavable Thanksgiving dinner in college about ten years ago, and that one experience was enough to shape our thoughts on the product. They just aren't good. At all. To get prepared, all we did was peruse the offerings in the frozen-food aisle, which made us realize how unbelievably easy it would be to make literally anything taste better than those little frozen cardboard packages masquerading as good food. So, we bring to you the TV dinner classics you think you remember in a way that you have never imagined.

4
les
CLASSIQUES

PAGE 65

Bonsoir mon ami! Bienvenue dans le monde de la cuisine française! French food has always had a reputation for being complex, time-consuming to prepare, and intimidating. And often, it really is. While a perfect French soufflé is tricky to master, classic doesn't need to mean hard. A PB&J is classic and you learned how to make that when you were a four-year-old. This chapter contains reinterpretations of some French classics that span the difficulty spectrum between a soufflé and a PB&J. So although you may recognize the titles, these are going to be easier, more accessible versions, with a few shortcuts here and there to help you "master the art."

5
future CLASSICS

PAGE 87

When your own children are grown up, there will be virtual-reality grocery shopping via Google glasses synced to the family's personal drone. But hopefully, sitting down to dinner as a family will still exist. And if they need some inspiration to whip up dinner, this chapter is for them. In these recipes, we've mashed up some old flavors with some newfangled techniques to create dishes that, in years to come, will be immortalized as classics.

6
worldwide CLASSICS

PAGE 109

While every kid wishes he or she could do like Peter Pan in *Hook* and conjure up big bowls of colorful whipped cream, perfectly crisp turkey legs, and endless pies via his or her imagination, what every kid gets stuck eating is pretty much the same local cuisine over and over. Whether it's some kind of chicken, a bean stew, or braised meat, it's usually a protein with potatoes, noodles, or rice. But world cuisine doesn't need to be only that. Like seeing your favorite artist in a stadium, there are the classics you know you'll hear and the songs you pray will be played. We didn't want to reinterpret the ones that everyone already knows all the words to and sing along. So we dug a bit deeper—for the song that gets played every four concerts and makes the crowd go absolutely wild.

7
breakfast CLASSICS

PAGE 125

A perfectly cooked egg is the artistic equivalent to Rembrandt painting da Vinci's *Mona Lisa* in the style of Picasso. If you can fry an egg sunny-side up to just the right temperature and temperament, the sheen of the yolk and the glisten of the white will be so captivating that you may need to invest in velvet ropes to keep the throngs of picture-snapping tourists away from the beautiful masterpiece you've created for the world. This chapter of breakfast dishes will take you from your current skill level (Denny's short-order cook) to full-fledged breakfast artiste.

8
sweet CLASSICS

PAGE 139

No chapter for this book inspired a more aggressive response than when we crowdsourced options for classic desserts to reimagine. When it comes to sweets, people really freak out. Everyone always wants to take a peek at the dessert menu at the end of the meal. So we put our desserts at the end of the book for some guilt-free viewing. We were warned that messing with classic desserts was dangerous territory. "Why change things that are already delicious?" people asked. "To make them better than the original!" we answered. Obviously. Since we aren't classically trained pastry chefs, what follows are some incredible variations on favorite desserts that are mindbogglingly good and easy for a home cook to execute. And while the recipe names sound familiar and appear normal, don't be fooled. These are not the corner-diner cake or your grandma's pie.

WITH SPECIAL FEATURES ON:

FROM GENERATION TO GENERATION,

certain foods are passed down—foods so timeless that neither the changing world nor any culinary Zeitgeist can shake them from our forks. We enjoy gnocchi now as much as a donkey herder did in Sicily two hundred years ago. A bite of cheesecake is as delicious today as it was to a group of day-drunk women having lunch on Park Avenue half a century ago. We will never abandon these classic dishes, because we find comfort in how unchanged they are in a world where change is constant and undeniable. *Damn, that was beautiful.*

And then there are the foods that people enjoyed in the past that were insanely disgusting and that, thank god, we don't eat anymore. For every timeless dish that we celebrate, some ten gnarly ones have been long forgotten. In the 1950s, people **loved** eating everything in Jell-O. Tuna salad in a lime Jell-O mold was a dish that you would proudly serve to those you loved. In the 1970s, people frequently ate a dish called "bananas hollandaise," which consisted of bananas with slices of hot ham on top, covered in—you guessed it—hollandaise sauce. As a child, I can remember my grandmother telling me that she relished a dessert called "vinegar pie," which was **a pie that tasted like vinegar**. I'm not even trying to be dramatic here, but she might as well have told me that eating scabs was her favorite snack, because that's how repulsed my nine-year-old self was at the thought of a vinegar pie. And I still feel that way today. *Nobody should ever eat that dessert again.*

It makes sense, though: it's survival of the fittest for food—survival of the foodest. *(Sorry, that was bad.)* The tastiest stuff sticks around, and the old-timey barf stuff falls into the rearview mirror of yesteryear. But the system isn't perfect, and every so often it experiences a glitch, leaving tasty awesomeness in the past.

THAT'S WHERE THE SUSSMAN BROTHERS COME IN.

They are both Marty McFly from *Back to the Future*, two hunks with great bone structure and cool shoes reaching back in time to change the course of history. *Oh, is that too much? Too bad, this is my foreword, so I'll say whatever I want. If I want to talk about the dots on Morgan Freeman's face and not food, I can do that. Okay, sorry, where was I?* With their restaurants and their books, the Sussman boys are trying to make things right, to correct our historical culinary mistakes. Like who decided that we no longer eat fondue? Why would dipping fruit and bread into a pot of cheese or chocolate ever become passé? Why did gin become an afterthought? Gin was the preferred drink of tough guys who could kick your ass, guys who had beards at age fifteen and built stuff with their bare hands. This book begs us to reconsider both fondue and gin—and countless other dishes and drinks—and induct them into the Tastiness Hall of Fame, where they rightfully belong.

These culinary Magellans have a heavy burden on their shoulders, as it is never easy to rewrite history. But if anyone is up to the challenge, it is Max and Eli, because they are cool. *After all, they chose me to write a foreword for their book, didn't they?*

— JOSH OSTROVSKY, *aka* "THE FAT JEW" *aka* "FATRICK JEWING"

Ol' Blue Eyes, a 1963 Corvette, a tailored suit, a dry-aged rib eye, Led Zeppelin, Tom Cruise in *Risky Business*—some things are untouchably classic. They work perfectly the way they are, regardless of what iterations came afterward. Recipes, however, should be ever expanding and evolving. We believe that a dish—no matter how classic and iconic—has the ability to morph into something new and fantastic. So operating with the idea that no food, technique, preparation, or flavor combination is set in stone, and embracing evolution as a good thing, we're back to reimagine our choice collection of classic dishes.

In our minds, there isn't anything sacred about food except that it should taste amazing. No recipe should be overly complicated to cook. As you can see from the cover photo, we got dressed up and went all old-time classic good on you. But don't be intimidated by how incredibly handsome we look or how monumentally tasty the food appears. Yes, yes . . . we look amazing. And yes, the food in this cookbook looks incredible and is absurdly tasty. But the point is, you can cook all of this stuff. All of it. We've reinvented, rejiggered, reordered, and re-created all of these classics so you can sink your teeth right into them, literally and figuratively.

So crank up the *Stairway to Heaven*, pop on some Ray-Bans, strip down to your underwear and socks, and slide into the kitchen. It's time to get cooking.

1

CLASSICS
from our
CHILDHOOD

RECIPES BASED ON FOOD WE ATE GROWING UP

TEMPURA ASPARAGUS
with chinese broccoli

Asparagus was the vegetable we most commonly ate growing up. Here, a bed of leafy Chinese broccoli provides an excellent textural contrast to the crispy tempura asparagus. The Sichuan-inspired sauce, a perfect mix of slightly sweet and sticky, brings the entire dish together. This dish is nothing like what our mom made, but she's the queen of creative license, so we're following suit.

tempura batter

¾ cup (4 oz/125 g) all-purpose flour

3 Tbsp cornstarch

Pinch of kosher salt

About 1 cup (8 fl oz/250 ml) soda water

2 cups (16 fl oz/500 ml) chicken stock

¼ cup (1 oz/30 g) fermented black beans

1 Tbsp soy sauce

1 tsp Chinese five-spice powder

1 tsp freshly ground Sichuan peppercorns

1 Tbsp cornstarch dissolved in 3 Tbsp water

Kosher salt

4 cups (32 fl oz/1 l) vegetable oil, plus 1 Tbsp

1 leek, white and tender green parts only, cut into rounds

1 lb (500 g) Chinese broccoli (*gai lan*), ends trimmed, leaves roughly torn, and stems cut into 1-inch (2.5-cm) batons

1 small red jalapeño chile, seeded and sliced

1 bunch asparagus, ends trimmed, spears halved crosswise

Sea salt

1 bunch green onions, white and tender green parts only, sliced on the diagonal

To make the tempura batter, in a bowl, whisk together the flour, cornstarch, and kosher salt. Whisk in the soda water, a little at a time, until the batter is the consistency of a thin paste; you may not need all of the soda water. The batter should be slightly lumpy and just barely coat a spoon. Let the batter rest in the refrigerator for at least 10 minutes and up to 2 hours before using.

In a small saucepan, combine the stock, black beans, soy sauce, five-spice powder, and ground peppercorns and bring to a boil over high heat. Whisk together the cornstarch mixture briefly to recombine, then whisk it into the boiling stock mixture. The sauce will thicken. Taste and adjust the seasoning with kosher salt. Remove from the heat and cover to keep warm.

In a large saucepan, heat the 4 cups (32 fl oz/1 l) vegetable oil over medium-high heat to 350°F (180°C). Line a baking sheet with paper towels.

While the oil is heating, in a deep frying pan, heat the 1 tablespoon vegetable oil over high heat. Add the leek and sauté until deep golden brown, about 3 minutes. Add the broccoli and jalapeño and stir-fry until they begin to color slightly, about 3 minutes. Remove from the heat and keep warm.

One at a time, coat the asparagus pieces with the batter, allowing any excess to drip off. Working in batches to prevent crowding, and holding the asparagus just above the surface of the oil to prevent splattering, gently drop the pieces into the hot oil. Adjust the batter with more flour or soda water if necessary to achieve a crispy exterior; if too thin, the result will be greasy. Fry until golden brown, 2–3 minutes. Using a slotted spoon, transfer the asparagus to the prepared baking sheet and sprinkle lightly with sea salt. Repeat with the remaining asparagus.

To serve, place a layer of the broccoli on a plate, top with some of the asparagus, and drizzle the sauce over the asparagus. Garnish with the green onions and serve right away.

detroit
GREEK SALAD

The Detroit Coney Island–style Greek salad is a thing of simple beauty. Iceberg lettuce, beefsteak tomatoes, and cukes provide crisp freshness, and the dressing and olives deliver the acid that every dish needs. It's a hearty, working-class salad that everyone can love. Not too stuffy, not too cute. Just damn tasty. So how to improve on such an iconic Coney classic? Sometimes it's the small things in life—like a deep-fried cube of feta cheese and roasted tomatoes—that can just make everything right in the world.

6 plum tomatoes, quartered lengthwise

½ cup (4 fl oz/125 ml) plus 1 Tbsp extra-virgin olive oil

Kosher salt

¼ cup (1½ oz/45 g) all-purpose flour

2 large eggs, beaten

¼ cup (⅓ oz/10 g) panko bread crumbs

½ lb (250 g) feta cheese, cut into 1½-inch (4-cm) pieces

3 Tbsp red wine vinegar

1 head green leaf or baby red leaf lettuce, leaves separated

½ cup (2½ oz/75 g) pitted Kalamata olives

1 or 2 beets, boiled until tender, peeled, and cut into wedges

½ red onion, thinly sliced

1 cucumber, cut into ½-inch (12-mm) dice

Preheat the oven to 375°F (190°C).

In a bowl, toss the tomatoes with 2 tablespoons of the olive oil and ½ teaspoon salt. Transfer to a rimmed baking sheet. Roast until the tomatoes are dark brown, have dried out on the outside, and are slightly leathery, about 45 minutes. Set aside.

Meanwhile, put the flour, eggs, and panko into separate bowls. A few at a time, toss the feta pieces in the flour, then coat with the eggs, and finally coat completely with the panko, shaking off the excess after each step. Refrigerate until ready to fry.

In a blender or food processor, combine half of the tomatoes, 5 tablespoons (3 fl oz/ 80 ml) of the olive oil, the vinegar, and ½ teaspoon salt and blend until smooth. Set the vinaigrette aside.

In a frying pan, heat the remaining 2 tablespoons olive oil over medium heat. When the oil is hot, add the feta and cook, turning as needed, until golden brown on all sides, about 3 minutes. Transfer to paper towels to drain.

In a large bowl, toss together the lettuce, olives, beets, onion, cucumber, the remaining tomatoes, and the vinaigrette. Garnish with the feta. Serve right away.

CRISPY ARTICHOKES
with miso aioli

From a young age, we've been kitchen loiterers—picking, tasting, snacking. Our mom *loves* artichokes, and she is the first to admit she's full-on addicted. When we were young, she would boil whole artichokes and we'd dip the leaves in a lemony mayo. They were *for* dinner, but they were always gone wayyyyy before we even sat down for dinner. These crispy ones are so amazing that we're sure they will never hit the table. There's nothing wrong with that.

miso aioli
2 large egg yolks

2 Tbsp white miso

2 Tbsp rice vinegar

1½ cups (12 fl oz/375 ml) vegetable oil

Ice water, if needed

Kosher salt and freshly ground pepper

2 Tbsp extra-virgin olive oil

1 can (14 oz/440 g) artichoke hearts, drained and patted dry

¼ cup (¼ oz/7 g) fresh cilantro leaves

To make the aioli, in a food processor, combine the egg yolks, miso, and vinegar and process just until blended. With the processor running, drizzle in the vegetable oil in a slow, steady stream until the mixture is emulsified. If the aioli is too thick, thin it slightly with ice water. Season with salt and pepper. Transfer the aioli to a small bowl, cover, and refrigerate until ready to serve.

In a large sauté pan, heat the olive oil over high heat. When the oil is shimmering, add the artichoke hearts (be careful, as the oil will splatter) and cook, turning once, until they are heated through and crispy on the outside, 3–4 minutes.

Serve the artichokes right away, garnished with the cilantro and accompanied with the aioli.

our dad's
LAMB STEW

Every Passover our father makes a rich lamb stew. Passover seders are no joke at our parents' house and can stretch long into the night. So by the time the lamb hits the table, we're so hungry that it seems like we've never eaten before in our lives. This dish takes all the flavors of that stew and condenses them into a sauce that accompanies the lamb chops. Slightly more refined, same intensely delicious flavor. And we won't make you suffer through the ten plagues (and ten hours of singing) in order to eat it.

marinade

4 anchovy fillets, mashed with a fork

Grated zest and juice of 1 orange

2 garlic cloves, crushed

1/2 tsp red pepper flakes

2 Tbsp extra-virgin olive oil

1/2 tsp *each* fresh oregano leaves and dried Mexican oregano

2 Tbsp whole-milk Greek yogurt

2 tsp kosher salt

4 lamb rib chops, each 2 inches (5 cm) thick

1 tsp cumin seeds

4 Tbsp (2 fl oz/60 ml) extra-virgin olive oil

1 small red onion, chopped

1/2 tsp ground turmeric

2 garlic cloves, minced

1 plum tomato, chopped

1 can (15 1/2 oz/485 g) chickpeas, rinsed and drained

3 cups (24 fl oz/750 ml) chicken stock

2 handfuls chopped greens such as kale, mustard greens, or Swiss chard

1/2 cup (3 oz/90 g) *each* chopped dried apricots and pitted dates

1 small jalapeño chile, minced

Kosher salt and freshly ground pepper

1 lemon for zesting

To make the marinade, in a bowl, mix together the anchovy fillets, orange zest, orange juice, garlic, red pepper flakes, olive oil, both oreganos, yogurt, and salt. Put the lamb chops in a baking dish, add the marinade, and turn the chops to coat evenly. Refrigerate for at least 2 hours or up to overnight.

Let the lamb chops come to room temperature for 1 hour before cooking them.

Meanwhile, in a saucepan, toast the cumin seeds over medium-high heat until fragrant and barely smoking, 2–3 minutes. Add 2 tablespoons of the olive oil, the onion, and the turmeric and sauté until softened, about 4 minutes. Add the garlic and tomato and sauté until softened, 3–5 minutes. Add the chickpeas and stock and simmer over low heat until the chickpeas are tender, about 10 minutes.

Fold in the greens, apricots, dates, and jalapeño and simmer for 5 minutes. Taste and adjust the seasoning if necessary. Remove from the heat and cover to keep warm.

Preheat the broiler. Scrape the marinade off the surface of the lamb chops. Season the chops lightly with 1 teaspoon each kosher salt and pepper.

In a broiler-safe, heavy-bottomed frying pan, heat the remaining 2 tablespoons olive oil over medium-high heat. Add the chops and cook for 1–2 minutes on each side, moving them as needed to ensure even contact and browning. Transfer the pan to the broiler and cook for 2 minutes. Flip the chops and cook on the other side for 2 minutes. An instant-read thermometer inserted into the thickest part of a chop, away from the bone, should register 130°F (54°C) for medium-rare.

Divide the stewed chickpeas among individual plates and top each with a lamb chop. Grate the zest of the lemon over the top and serve right away.

"GEFILTE" fish terrine

For Passover, our aunts Beth and Eve, along with our mom and nana, make gefilte fish, a family tradition. It's a tremendously laborious process with the end result that our entire house smells like boiled fish for two days, which is . . . tradition! Yeah, tradition! This take on our family's gefilte fish is a terrine topped with smoked salmon, yielding a more beautiful layered dish that will have your guests asking which French chef trained you and not asking which fish market exploded in your living room.

1 Tbsp extra-virgin olive oil

1 large white onion, finely diced

³/₄ lb (375 g) fresh salmon fillet, cut into chunks

³/₄ lb (375 g) carp or pike fillet, cut into chunks

1 carrot, peeled and shredded

Grated zest of 2 lemons

1 tsp fresh lemon juice

2 large eggs, beaten

2 Tbsp matzo meal

1 tsp kosher salt

1 tsp freshly ground pepper

1 Tbsp chopped fresh dill

¹/₄ lb (125 g) smoked salmon

1 bunch arugula

1 jar (12 oz/375 g) piquillo peppers, drained

Preheat the oven to 325°F (165°C). Line the bottom and sides of a 9-by-5-inch (23-by-13-cm) loaf pan or terrine dish with plastic wrap.

In a small frying pan, heat the olive oil over medium heat. Add the onion and cook, stirring occasionally, until softened, about 8 minutes. Set aside.

In a food processor, combine the fresh salmon and carp and pulse until finely chopped but not smooth (the mixture should not form a paste). Transfer to a large bowl and add the onion, carrot, lemon zest, lemon juice, eggs, matzo meal, ¾ cup (6 fl oz/180 ml) cold water, the salt, and the pepper. Stir until well combined, then fold in the dill.

Transfer the fish mixture to the prepared pan and cover with parchment paper. Place the pan in a roasting pan and pour boiling water into the roasting pan to within 1 inch (2.5 cm) of the rim of the loaf pan. Transfer to the oven and bake until a skewer or thin knife blade inserted into the center of the terrine comes out clean or an instant-read thermometer inserted into the center registers 160°F (71°C), about 45 minutes.

Remove the roasting pan from the oven, then remove the loaf pan from the roasting pan. Let the terrine cool until room temperature. Peel off the parchment paper covering the terrine, invert a plate on top of the pan, and then invert the pan and plate together. Lift off the pan and peel away the plastic wrap. Use a paper towel to absorb any excess liquid on the plate, then cover the terrine with plastic wrap and refrigerate for 1 hour.

Meanwhile, dice the smoked salmon, arugula, and piquillo peppers and stir together in a bowl.

Top the terrine with the smoked salmon mixture, then cut into slices and serve.

SALMON
with chermoula &
SAUTÉED VEGETABLES

This recipe is based on our mom's oven-broiled salmon. We've updated it with *chermoula*, a North African marinade we love, here adapted as a sauce. You'll be cooking the salmon directly in a pot of oil, eliminating the possibility of a dry end result. The key to the vegetables is to let them get a lot of color (aka brown crispy bits), which makes them much tastier.

chermoula

1 cup (1½ oz/45 g) *each* chopped fresh cilantro leaves and stems and flat-leaf parsley leaves

½ cup (4 fl oz/125 ml) extra-virgin olive oil

Kosher salt

1 tsp *each* ground cumin and sweet Spanish paprika

¼ tsp *each* ground coriander and cayenne pepper

4 garlic cloves, minced

About ¼ cup (2 fl oz/60 ml) ice water

½ cup (4 oz/125 g) whole-milk Greek yogurt

salmon

4 cups (32 fl oz/1 l) extra-virgin olive oil, plus more if needed

2 salmon fillets, each about 6 oz (185 g)

Kosher salt and freshly ground pepper

Coarse sea salt

vegetables

2 Tbsp extra-virgin olive oil

1 cup (6 oz/185 g) cherry tomatoes, halved

½ red onion, diced

1 *each* zucchini and yellow squash, sliced

Pinch of kosher salt

2 tsp unsalted butter

¼ cup (⅓ oz/10 g) *each* chopped fresh flat-leaf parsley and cilantro

To make the chermoula, in a blender, combine the cilantro, parsley, olive oil, 1 tablespoon kosher salt, the cumin, paprika, coriander, cayenne, and garlic and blend until smooth. Add enough ice water to make a smooth emulsion. Transfer to a bowl and fold in the yogurt until combined. Taste and adjust the seasoning. Set aside until serving or cover and refrigerate for up to overnight.

To make the salmon, in a pot just large enough to fit the salmon, heat the olive oil over medium heat to 250°F (120°C). Season the fish with kosher salt and pepper. Submerge in the hot oil, adding a little more oil if needed to cover the salmon completely. Cook, stirring gently once or twice, until an instant-read thermometer inserted into the thickest part of the fish registers 125°F (52°C) for medium-rare, 5–7 minutes, or until done to your liking. Using a slotted spoon or fish spatula, transfer the salmon to a plate and pat with paper towels to remove excess oil. Sprinkle with sea salt.

To make the vegetables, in a cast-iron or other heavy-bottomed frying pan, heat the olive oil over high heat. When the oil is nearly smoking, add the tomatoes, onion, squashes, and kosher salt. Cook without disturbing until the vegetables are deeply caramelized on the first side, about 2 minutes, then toss gently and cook until the vegetables are tender, about 2 minutes longer. Add the butter, parsley, and cilantro and toss to combine.

To serve, spoon a pool of the chermoula on each plate, spoon some vegetables to the side, and place a salmon fillet on top of the chermoula. Serve right away.

brisket & potato
KUGEL

If you've ever seen a *baleboste* serve a meal, you know when you pass your plate down, you're getting "a *bissel*" (Yiddish for "a little taste") of everything, whether you want it or not. When we were growing up, we often noticed that, due to lack of space on the dinner plate, the crispy kugel would always share real estate with a hefty portion of braised brisket. So we thought, maybe put a *bissel* of dis inside a *bissel* of dat? Have a nosh of it? We tasted, and *oy vey iz mir!* So good we nearly *plotzed*.

brisket

1 Tbsp extra-virgin olive oil

2 lb (1 kg) beef brisket, cut into 1-inch (2.5-cm) pieces

Pinch of kosher salt

1 yellow onion, finely diced

1 garlic clove, minced

1 tsp firmly packed light brown sugar

1 Tbsp tomato paste

2 cups (16 fl oz/500 ml) chicken stock

Pinch of red pepper flakes

⅓ cup (3 fl oz/80 ml) vegetable oil

Kosher salt

3 lb (1.5 kg) russet potatoes, peeled and cut into 2-inch (5-cm) pieces

1 yellow onion, minced

7 large eggs, beaten

1 tsp freshly ground pepper

To make the brisket, in a wide pot, heat the olive oil over high heat. When the oil is very hot, add the brisket and salt and cook, stirring, until browned, about 5 minutes. Reduce the heat to medium, add the onion, and sauté until the onion is softened and caramelized, about 7 minutes. Add the garlic, brown sugar, and tomato paste and sauté for 3–4 minutes. Add the stock and red pepper flakes and bring to a simmer. Reduce the heat to low, cover, and simmer until the meat is falling apart and tender, 2–3 hours. Add water if the pan begins to dry. The meat should be just barely covered with liquid when it is ready. If there is too much liquid at the end, transfer the liquid to a small saucepan and simmer over medium-high heat until reduced. Set the brisket aside.

Pour the vegetable oil into a 9-by-13-inch (23-by-33-cm) baking pan and place in the oven. Preheat the oven to 375°F (190°C).

Meanwhile, bring a large pot of salted water to a boil over high heat. Add the potatoes and cook for 3 minutes. Drain in a colander and rinse under cold running water.

Working in batches, pulse the potatoes in a food processor, leaving them slightly chunky, with pieces no larger than ¼ inch (6 mm). (Be careful not to overprocess, or they will be gluey.) Transfer to a large bowl and add the onion, eggs, 1 tablespoon salt, and the pepper.

Remove the pan from the oven and spoon in half of the potato mixture, spreading it evenly to the edges of the pan. Spread the brisket evenly on top, then cover with the remaining potatoes.

Bake until the potatoes are tender and the top is crispy, about 1½ hours. Let cool slightly before serving.

ROASTED CHICKEN
with wild mushrooms & tagliatelle

One of the classic dishes in the Lynne Avadenka (our mom) repertoire was chicken breasts with a cremini mushroom sauce and egg noodles. We spent many a Shabbat dinner eating this scrumptious concoction (which Eli always liked best cold the next day). Using our mom's recipe as the inspiration, we've swapped in a whole roasted chicken, which will look beautiful on the table (easy to cook but looks hard—show-off points for you), and we serve it with whole-wheat tagliatelle (very healthy!). Woodsy mushrooms add an earthy flavor and allow you to embrace your inner farm-to-table forager.

6 Tbsp (3 oz/90 g) unsalted butter, at room temperature

Leaves from 2 fresh rosemary sprigs

Leaves from 3 fresh thyme sprigs

1 whole chicken, about 3 lb (1.5 kg)

2 tablespoons extra-virgin olive oil, plus more if needed

Kosher salt and freshly ground pepper

1 cup (8 fl oz/250 ml) chicken stock

1 small yellow onion, diced

½ lb (250 g) button mushrooms, brushed clean and halved

½ lb (250 g) cremini mushrooms, brushed clean and halved

¼ lb (125 g) porcini or king oyster mushrooms, brushed clean and thinly sliced

¼ lb (125 g) oyster mushrooms, brushed clean and halved

1 lb (500 g) dried whole-wheat tagliatelle

Preheat the oven to 375°F (190°C).

In a small bowl, stir together 4 tablespoons (2 oz/60 g) of the butter, the rosemary, and the thyme. Using your fingers, gently loosen the skin covering the breast and thighs of the chicken, rub the flesh with the butter mixture, and then pat the skin back into place. Rub the outside of the chicken with the 2 tablespoons olive oil. Sprinkle with salt and pepper.

Place the chicken, breast side up, in a roasting pan and roast for 45 minutes, basting it halfway through with the stock. If the skin is not golden brown after 45 minutes, raise the oven temperature to 450°F (230°C) and roast for 5 minutes longer. To test for doneness, insert an instant-read thermometer into the thickest part of a thigh, away from the bone; it should register 165°F (74°C).

Transfer the chicken to a cutting board, tent with aluminum foil, and let rest for about 10 minutes before carving. Transfer the cooking juices to a clear measuring cup and skim off the fat and reserve. Reserve the juices.

In a large nonstick frying pan, warm 1 tablespoon of the reserved fat over medium heat. Add the onion and cook, stirring occasionally, until it begins to turn golden brown, about 10 minutes. Transfer to a small bowl. Wipe out the pan with paper towels.

In the same pan, heat 2 more tablespoons of the reserved fat over high heat (add olive oil if you do not have enough chicken fat). Add the mushrooms and cook, stirring frequently so they do not burn, until browned, 3–5 minutes. Add 1 tablespoon of the butter and cook until browned and foamy and the mushrooms are tender, about 3 minutes. Return the onion to the pan, pour in 1 cup (8 fl oz/250 ml) of the reserved juices, stir in the remaining 1 tablespoon butter, and heat through.

Meanwhile, bring a large pot of salted water to a boil over high heat. Add the pasta and cook until al dente according to the package directions. Drain the pasta.

Carve the chicken and serve the mushroom sauce over the pasta and the chicken.

The only thing

MORE COMFORTING THAN A BOWL OF

WARM SOUP

IS A HUG FROM YOUR MOM.

Those canned-soup ads really know how to get to you. They elicit old memories of when you were home sick and your mom made you chicken noodle soup, and even though you were nearly dying, *The Price Is Right,* a bowl of soup, and some reassuring words would turn the whole thing around. So here are three recipes, plus a basic chicken stock that you can use to make them: a trio of reimagined classics from three different cultures, all of them with that comforting "hug from mom" flavor.

CHICKEN SOUP IS THE

gateway drug of Jewish food.

You may have never eaten chopped chicken liver, but you've almost certainly had chicken soup with a matzo ball. And a good chicken soup demands a good chicken stock. A first-rate stock is close to our hearts because not only is it important to much of Jewish cuisine but also to hundreds of other ethnic dishes. So, once you have mastered stock, you can make tons of other soups and sauces from just that starting point. And what goes with all of those soups? Crusty toasted bread, a baguette, a loaf of sourdough, tortillas, pita chips. It doesn't really matter which one you choose as long as you can use it either to dip into or to

SOP UP EVERY LAST DELICIOUS BIT OF THE SOUP.

CHICKEN STOCK

6 lb (3 kg) chicken bones

2 lb (1 kg) carrots, chopped

1 bunch celery, heart and ribs chopped

2 large white onions, halved

1 bay leaf

1 head garlic, halved

1 bunch fresh flat-leaf parsley

1 bunch fresh dill

Kosher salt and freshly ground pepper

makes about 4 qt (4 l)

This is the starting point for the three super filling soups that follow. Do this first step correctly and everything you use the result for will be scrumptious. As any bubby, saucier, or ramen master will tell you, it all begins with the stock.

Put the chicken bones in a large stockpot and add water to cover (about 5 qt/5 l). Bring to a simmer over high heat, then reduce the heat to medium and simmer, uncovered, for about 40 minutes, skimming off any fat and impurities that form on the surface. Add the carrots, celery, onions, bay leaf, garlic, parsley, and dill, reduce the heat to low, and simmer, uncovered, for about 2 hours.

Strain the stock through a fine-mesh sieve into a large bowl and discard the solids. Season the stock with salt and pepper.

Let the stock cool, uncovered, then transfer to storage containers, cover, and refrigerate for up to 4 days or freeze for up to 6 months. Lift off any fat solidified on the surface before using.

PORK & KIMCHI SOUP

½ lb (250 g) pork shoulder, cut into ½-inch (12-mm) pieces

1 garlic clove, minced

1 Tbsp peeled and minced fresh ginger

Kosher salt

1 Tbsp vegetable oil

½ red onion, thinly sliced

1 cup (5 oz/155 g) drained kimchi, juice reserved

1½ cups (12 fl oz/375 ml) Chicken Stock (above)

About ¼ cup (2 fl oz/60 ml) kimchi juice

1 block (½ lb/250 g) firm tofu, cut into 1-inch (2.5-cm) cubes

1–2 Tbsp Korean chile paste (*gochujang*)

½ bunch green onions, white and tender green parts only, thinly sliced

Steamed rice for serving

serves 4

Kimchi, the national dish of Korea, is a traditional fermented side dish of vegetables and seasonings. It is most often made with napa cabbage. Although lots of variations exist, all have a pungent, spicy flavor that goes perfectly with meat. Here, the kimchi and the pork provide the backbone for a full-meal soup that is equal parts sour, funky, tangy, and hearty.

In a bowl, combine the pork, garlic, ginger, and 1 teaspoon salt and toss to coat the pork evenly. Cover and refrigerate for at least 30 minutes or up to overnight.

In a saucepan, heat the vegetable oil over high heat. Add the pork and cook, stirring, until nicely caramelized, about 5 minutes. Add the onion and sauté until slightly softened, 3–5 minutes. Add the kimchi, reduce the heat to medium, and simmer for 5 minutes.

Add the stock and kimchi juice and simmer until the pork is tender, about 45 minutes. Add the tofu and simmer until warmed through and slightly softened, 10–15 minutes. Stir in the chile paste. Taste and adjust the seasoning.

Add the green onions and serve right away, with rice on the side.

CHICKEN PHO

broth

2-inch (5-cm) piece lemongrass stalk, white part only

¼ cup (1¼ oz/40 g) peeled and chopped fresh ginger (1-inch/2.5-cm pieces)

1 head garlic, halved lengthwise

2 star anise pods

1 tsp fennel seeds

1 whole clove

8 cups (2 l) Chicken Stock (page 29)

1 bunch green onions, white and tender green parts only, roughly chopped

3 Tbsp fish sauce

3 Tbsp firmly packed light brown sugar

1 whole chicken, about 2½ lb (1.25 kg), cut into 8 pieces and skin removed

¾ lb (375 g) dried rice noodles

garnish

1 cup (1 oz/30 g) whole fresh cilantro leaves and minced stems

1 cup (1 oz/30 g) fresh Thai basil leaves

1 bunch green onions, white and tender green parts only, sliced on the diagonal

1 cup (3½ oz/105 g) bean sprouts

1 jalapeño chile, seeded and sliced

Hoisin sauce for serving (optional)

serves 4

While ramen is currently in the spotlight (Max is obsessed), pho, a Vietnamese classic containing rice noodles, beef or chicken, and herbs, is, after matzo ball soup, Eli's favorite soup. He likes to squeeze hoisin sauce into the rich broth to make it even sweeter. Even though this is chicken pho, there's nothing wrong with putting a little leftover hangar steak from page 53 or brisket from page 24 on top. Remember to get the traditional garnishes: cilantro, limes, Thai basil, bean sprouts, and red chiles!

To make the broth, place the lemongrass, ginger, garlic, star anise, fennel seeds, and clove on a piece of cheesecloth, gather the edges together, and tie securely with kitchen string. In a large saucepan, combine the stock, green onions, fish sauce, brown sugar, chicken, and cheesecloth bundle and bring to a simmer over high heat. Reduce the heat to low and cook for about 1 hour, skimming off and discarding any fat or impurities that form on the surface.

After 1 hour, remove and discard the cheesecloth bundle. Transfer the chicken to a cutting board. Let cool, then shred the meat, discarding the bones, and return the meat to the broth. Reheat until hot.

Meanwhile, cook the rice noodles according to the package directions and drain.

Ladle the soup into 4 bowls. Add the noodles, dividing them evenly. Garnish with the cilantro, basil, green onions, bean sprouts, and jalapeño and serve with the hoisin sauce, if using.

POSOLE WITH CHICKEN MEATBALLS

chicken meatballs

1 lb (500 g) ground chicken

1 large egg, lightly beaten

1 tsp garlic powder

1 tsp kosher salt

1 tsp ground coriander

1 tsp freshly ground white pepper

3 Tbsp panko bread crumbs

2 Tbsp vegetable oil

1 red onion, finely diced

4 garlic cloves, minced

1 can (16 oz/500 g) hominy, rinsed and drained

1 can (24 oz/750 g) whole tomatoes and their juices, puréed

2 plum tomatoes, diced

2 Tbsp ancho chile powder

2 Tbsp smoked paprika

1 Tbsp cayenne pepper

1 Tbsp ground cumin

2 dried árbol chiles

6 cups (48 fl oz/1.5 l) Chicken Stock (page 29)

1 cup (1½ oz/45 g) chopped fresh cilantro leaves and stems

2 limes, cut into wedges

serves 4

The term "posole" is used for both hominy (alkali-treated corn kernels) and for a Mexican soup made from hominy. Corn was a sacred plant to the Aztecs, which meant posole was reserved for special occasions. But we want you to make this new version any time. We've kept the flavoring here middle of the road, so that you can spice it up as you like. We love to eat the soup with crisp tortilla chips for dipping. If you've got chicharrones left over from making Mofongo (page 121), garnish with those!

To make the meatballs, in a bowl, combine the chicken, egg, garlic powder, salt, coriander, white pepper, and panko. Mix gently with your hands just until combined; do not overwork the meat. Form the mixture into meatballs about the size of golf balls.

In a nonstick frying pan, heat 1 tablespoon of the vegetable oil over medium heat. Add the meatballs and cook, turning as needed, until golden brown on the outside, about 8 minutes. Transfer to a plate.

In a large saucepan, heat the remaining 1 tablespoon vegetable oil over medium heat. Add the onion and sauté until it begins to wilt, about 5 minutes. Add the garlic, hominy, puréed tomatoes, diced tomatoes, chile powder, paprika, cayenne, cumin, and dried chiles and stir well. Add the stock and bring to a boil, then reduce the heat to low. Add the meatballs, stir well, and simmer uncovered, stirring occasionally, for 30 minutes. The meatballs should be cooked through and the flavors blended.

Divide the soup among individual bowls and garnish with the cilantro. Serve right away, with the lime wedges on the side.

2

CLASSICS
from your
CHILDHOOD

FOOD WE DIDN'T GROW UP EATING BUT OUR FRIENDS DID

sunday PASTA

The time it takes your *nonna* to make her Sunday pasta sauce is admirable. But let's face it, she's going to take that recipe to her grave. So why not bring together all of the best elements of the Italian combo sub, toss them into a pot, and then throw the fact that you don't need her recipe into your *nonna's* face! Wait, don't do that . . . your *nonna* is amazing and lovely and kind (but she's still never going to give you that recipe).

½ lb (250 g) sopressata, cut into 1-inch (2.5-cm) dice

½ lb (250 g) dry-cured ham or prosciutto (not thinly sliced), cut into 1-inch (2.5-cm) dice

½ lb pepperoni (not thinly sliced), cut into 1-inch (2.5-cm) dice

¼ cup (2 fl oz/60 ml) extra-virgin olive oil, plus 2 Tbsp

2 garlic cloves

2 cups (10 oz/315 g) finely diced carrot

2 cups (10 oz/315 g) finely diced yellow onion

2 cups (10 oz/315 g) finely diced celery

Kosher salt

½ lb (250 g) ground pork

1 cup (8 oz/250 g) tomato paste

4 fresh thyme sprigs

2 bay leaves

1 can (16 oz/500 g) crushed San Marzano or other good-quality tomatoes

3 cups (24 fl oz/750 ml) chicken stock

1 cup (8 fl oz/250 ml) dry white wine

1 tsp red pepper flakes, or more to taste

1 lb (500 g) large rigatoni

1 Tbsp unsalted butter

¾ cup (3 oz/90 g) grated aged provolone cheese

¼ lb (125 g) baby arugula

1 Tbsp aged balsamic vinegar

½ cup (2½ oz/75 g) sliced peperoncini

In a food processor, combine the sopressata, ham, and pepperoni and pulse until a coarse paste forms. Set aside.

In a large pot, heat the ¼ cup (2 fl oz/60 ml) olive oil over medium heat. Add the garlic, carrot, onion, celery, and 1 teaspoon salt. Reduce the heat to low, cover, and simmer, stirring regularly, until the vegetables are very soft, about 1 hour. Do not allow them to darken in color or burn.

Add the pork and the ground meat mixture, raise the heat to medium, and simmer, stirring often to prevent burning, for 30 minutes. Add the tomato paste, thyme, and bay leaves and reduce the heat to low. Stir in the crushed tomatoes and cook, stirring often, for 10 minutes. Add the stock, wine, and red pepper flakes and simmer, stirring occasionally to prevent sticking, until thick, about 30 minutes. Remove and discard the bay leaves.

When the sauce is almost done, bring a large pot of salted water to a boil over high heat. Add the pasta and cook for 1 minute less than the package directions for al dente. Drain the pasta (do not rinse) and reserve 1 cup (8 fl oz/250 ml) of the cooking water.

Return the pasta to the cooking pot and add the sauce, ½ cup (4 fl oz/125 ml) of the reserved cooking water, the butter, and half of the cheese. Place the pot over medium heat and heat, stirring, until the pasta is well coated with the sauce; if the pasta is dry, add more cooking water.

Transfer the pasta to a large serving platter. In a small bowl, mix together the arugula, the 2 tablespoons olive oil, the vinegar, the peperoncini, and the remaining cheese. Garnish the pasta with the arugula mixture and serve right away.

FRANKS 'N' BEANS

Franks 'n' beans is known as a gross slapdash meal made on the cheap and easy when money and creativity have run dry. Opening a can of beans and heating up a few chopped-up hot dogs is truthfully one of the lowest forms of human consumption, right above cup o' noodles on the lameness scale. Unless you are a cowboy, it's a meal you should avoid . . . until we created this version. This composed dish masquerading as franks 'n' beans is actually white beans and kale with caramelized onions, all spiced with chorizo. Giddyup.

1 Tbsp extra-virgin olive oil

½ lb (250 g) fresh chorizo, crumbled into ½-inch (12-mm) pieces

1 jalapeño chile, seeded and thinly sliced

1 garlic clove, thinly sliced

1 red onion, thinly julienned

1 bunch curly kale, stems and tough central spines removed and leaves torn into 2-inch (5-cm) pieces (about 6 cups/200 g)

Kosher salt

⅓ cup (3 fl oz/80 ml) chicken stock

1 can (15 oz/470 g) Great Northern beans or other white beans, rinsed and drained

Juice of 1 lemon

In a sauté pan, heat the olive oil over medium-high heat. Add the chorizo, jalapeño, garlic, and onion and cook, stirring frequently, until the onion caramelizes and the chorizo is almost cooked through, about 10 minutes.

Add the kale, a pinch of salt, and the stock, reduce the heat to medium-low, and cook, stirring occasionally, until the kale is tender, about 5 minutes.

Add the beans and lemon juice and heat, stirring occasionally, until warmed through. Taste and adjust the seasoning.

Spoon into individual bowls and serve right away.

arroz con pollo
ARANCINI

Show us something that isn't tasty when rolled into a ball, breaded, and deep-fried and we'll give you a $2 bill made entirely of real money. That's the wager. Take it or leave it.

¼ cup (2 fl oz/60 ml) extra-virgin olive oil

½ yellow onion, finely diced

2 boneless, skinless chicken thighs, cut into ½-inch (1-cm) pieces

½ cup (2½ oz/75 g) finely diced carrot

½ cup (2½ oz/75 g) finely diced red bell pepper

1 jalapeño chile, seeded and finely diced

1 garlic clove, minced

¾ cup (5½ oz/170 g) jasmine rice

1 Tbsp unsalted butter

1¼ cups (10 fl oz/310 ml) chicken stock

Kosher salt

1 bunch fresh cilantro, leaves chopped and stems minced

1 cup (5 oz/155 g) crumbled queso fresco

1 cup (5 oz/155 g) all-purpose flour

2 large eggs, beaten

1 cup (1½ oz/45 g) panko bread crumbs

salsa verde mayonnaise

2 jalapeño chiles, seeded

2 tomatillos, husked, rinsed, and halved

1 bunch fresh cilantro

1 garlic clove

½ avocado, pitted, peeled, and quartered

Kosher salt

1 Tbsp extra-virgin olive oil

1 Tbsp mayonnaise

Vegetable oil for deep-frying

In a large saucepan, heat the olive oil over medium heat. Add the onion, chicken, carrot, bell pepper, jalapeño, and garlic and cook, stirring occasionally, until very soft and the chicken is tender and fully cooked, about 30 minutes. Add the rice and butter and cook, stirring often, until the rice is fragrant, about 5 minutes.

Add the stock and 1 teaspoon salt and bring to a boil. Reduce the heat to low, cover, and simmer for 10 minutes. Remove from the heat and let stand for 30 minutes. Fluff the rice with a fork and let stand until cool enough to handle. Transfer the rice to a bowl, add the cilantro and queso fresco, and toss to combine. Taste and adjust the seasoning with salt.

Form the rice mixture into balls the size of Ping-Pong balls, using about 2 tablespoons for each one.

Put the flour, eggs, and panko into separate bowls. One at a time, dredge the rice balls in the flour, then coat with the eggs, and finally toss to coat well with the panko, shaking off any excess after each step. As the balls are breaded, place them on a baking sheet. Refrigerate the balls until ready to fry.

To make the mayonnaise, in a food processor, combine the jalapeños, tomatillos, cilantro, garlic, avocado, 1 teaspoon salt, the olive oil, ¼ cup (2 fl oz/60 ml) water, and the mayonnaise. Purée until smooth and blended. Transfer to a bowl. Taste and adjust the seasoning.

Pour the canola oil into a large, deep pot to a depth of 3 inches (7.5 cm) and heat to 350°F (180°C). Working in batches to avoid crowding, add the rice balls and fry until golden brown and heated through, 2–3 minutes. Using a slotted spoon, transfer to paper towels to drain.

Serve right away with the mayonnaise.

shellfish SHELLS

In the ocean, shells already have seafood inside them, and yes, those clams and oysters are often delicious as is. But what we realized was that shells in the ocean never come with tomato and cheese on them. (Ask any scientist, who will confirm that ocean shells are cheeseless and tomatoless.) So we drew on our friend's childhood love of his mom's baked pasta shells and made an even better, more delicious version by filling pasta shells with shrimp, clams, and tomatoes and baking them under a blanket of mozzarella. Guarantee Sue could make a killing selling these seashells by the seashore.

2 Tbsp extra-virgin olive oil

1 yellow onion, diced

2 garlic cloves, minced

¼ cup (2 fl oz/60 ml) dry white wine

1 can (28 oz/875 g) whole tomatoes, drained, then crushed or roughly puréed in a food processor

1 lb (500 g) shrimp, peeled, deveined, and minced

1 jar (6 oz/185 g) minced clams, drained

2 cups (1 lb/500 g) ricotta cheese

½ cup (¾ oz/20 g) panko bread crumbs, toasted

1 large egg, beaten

1 tsp red pepper flakes

½ tsp freshly ground black pepper

Kosher salt

½ cup (¾ oz/20 g) minced fresh flat-leaf parsley

35 jumbo pasta shells

1 cup (4 oz/125 g) shredded fresh mozzarella cheese

In a large sauté pan, heat the olive oil over medium heat. Add the onion and cook, stirring occasionally, until softened, about 5 minutes. Add the garlic and cook, stirring, for 1 minute. Add the wine and cook until reduced slightly, 3–4 minutes. Add the tomatoes and bring to a simmer. Transfer ¾ cup (6 fl oz/180 ml) of the sauce to a small bowl and set aside. Add the shrimp and clams to the sauce remaining in the pan and cook until the shrimp is just cooked through, 2–3 minutes. Remove from the heat and let cool.

Add the ricotta, panko, egg, red pepper flakes, black pepper, 1 teaspoon salt, and the parsley to the cooled seafood mixture and stir to combine. Cover and refrigerate until ready to use.

Preheat the oven to 375°F (190°C).

Bring a large pot of salted water to a boil over high heat. Add the pasta shells and cook until al dente, about 10 minutes, or according to the package directions. Drain and rinse the shells lightly. Using a spoon, fill the shells with the stuffing mixture, dividing it evenly. Place the shells in a 9-by-13-inch (23-by-33-cm) baking dish and dot them with the reserved tomato sauce (you don't need to cover them evenly with sauce), then sprinkle with the mozzarella.

Bake the shells until they are heated through and the cheese is melted, 20–25 minutes. Serve right away.

LINGUINE
tonnato

Tuna casserole. Just reading those words probably brings up awful memories from childhood. This flavorful linguine with Parmesan, bread crumbs, and tuna is nothing like tuna casserole. And that's the point. We're here to help you forget your grandma's casserole forever.

anchovy bread crumbs

2 Tbsp extra-virgin olive oil

4 anchovy fillets

1 cup (1½ oz/45 g) panko bread crumbs

1 garlic clove, minced

Grated zest of 1 lemon

2 Tbsp chopped fresh flat-leaf parsley

puréed tuna

1 can (4½ oz/140 g) Italian oil-packed tuna, drained

¼ cup (2 fl oz/60 ml) fresh lemon juice

1 garlic clove, minced

¼ cup (2 fl oz/60 ml) extra-virgin olive oil

1 tsp kosher salt

Kosher salt and freshly ground pepper

½ lb (250 g) dried linguine

1 Tbsp extra-virgin olive oil

1 garlic clove, roughly crushed

Kernels from 2 ears corn

1 cup (5 oz/155 g) shelled English peas

¼ cup (1 oz/30 g) grated Parmesan cheese

Juice of 1 lemon

To make the anchovy bread crumbs, in a nonstick frying pan, heat the olive oil over medium heat. Add the anchovy fillets and cook, mashing them with a small wooden spoon, until they fall apart, about 3 minutes. Add the panko and garlic and cook, tossing often, until golden brown, about 3 minutes. Transfer to paper towels to drain and cool, then toss with the lemon zest and parsley. Set aside.

To make the puréed tuna, in a blender or food processor, combine the tuna, lemon juice, garlic, olive oil, salt, and ¼ cup (2 fl oz/60 ml) water and purée until very smooth. Set aside.

Bring a pot of salted water to a boil over high heat. Add the pasta and cook for 1–2 minutes less than the package directions for al dente.

Meanwhile, in a large sauté pan, heat the olive oil over medium heat. Add the garlic and sauté until lightly golden brown, 3–5 minutes. Add the corn and peas and toss to warm through.

Drain the pasta (do not rinse), add to the sauté pan, and toss to combine. Add the puréed tuna, cheese, and lemon juice and toss again. Cook, stirring, until the ingredients are warmed through and the sauce is creamy, about 5 minutes.

Transfer to a serving bowl, garnish with the anchovy bread crumbs and pepper, and serve right away.

PORK CUTLETS
with sweet & spicy peppers

So your favorite foods growing up were pizza and chicken nuggets? That's cool. You should own your extremely boring, normal suburban childhood. And while you probably wish you could still eat those items every day, perhaps it's time to mature. These pork "nuggets" let you indulge in your childhood's greatest hits without having to shamefully cruise the frozen-food aisle.

2 pork tenderloins, each about 1 lb (500 g) and cut crosswise into 4 equal pieces

½ cup (2½ oz/75 g) all-purpose flour

2 large eggs, beaten

4 cups (6 oz/185 g) panko bread crumbs

¼ cup (2 fl oz/60 ml) extra-virgin olive oil

1 white onion, halved and sliced lengthwise

4 red bell peppers, seeded and cut into strips

4 green bell peppers, seeded and cut into strips

2 jalapeño chiles, seeded and cut into strips

2 Fresno chiles, seeded and cut into strips

4 garlic cloves

¼ cup (2 fl oz/60 ml) dry white wine

1 Tbsp dried oregano

1 Tbsp dried basil

2 Tbsp whole-grain mustard

¼ cup (2 fl oz/60 ml) vegetable oil

2 Tbsp unsalted butter

Kosher salt

Place a pork tenderloin piece between 2 sheets of plastic wrap. Using a mallet or a frying pan, pound the meat until it is ¼ inch (6 mm) thick. Repeat with the remaining pieces.

Put the flour, eggs, and panko into separate bowls. One at a time, dredge each pork cutlet in the flour, then coat with the eggs, and finally dredge in the panko, shaking off any excess after each step. Set aside.

In a sauté pan or large frying pan, heat the olive oil over medium heat. Add the onion and cook, without stirring, for 2 minutes to sear and brown slightly. Reduce the heat to low and add the bell peppers, jalapeño and Fresno chiles, and garlic. Cook, stirring gently every 5 minutes, so the vegetables release their liquid and begin to caramelize and soften. After 20 minutes, the vegetables should be soft. Add the wine and simmer until almost completely evaporated. Add the oregano, basil, and mustard and stir well. Remove the pan from the heat and cover to keep warm.

In a large frying pan, heat the vegetable oil over medium heat. Add 2 or 3 pork cutlets, making sure not to crowd the pan. Cook the cutlets, flipping them halfway through, until lightly browned on both sides, 3–4 minutes. Add 1 tablespoon of the butter to the pan, and when it begins to foam, use a spoon to baste the cutlets. Continue to baste, flipping the cutlets halfway through, until they are a deep golden brown on both sides, 3–4 minutes longer, for a total of 6–8 minutes cooking time. Transfer the cutlets to paper towels to drain. Sprinkle with salt and keep warm.

Top the cutlets with the spicy peppers and serve right away.

oxtail & goat cheese
TAMALES

We wanted to do a double-goat tamale, but goat meat still isn't that easy to find. So, in lieu of goat, we're using oxtail, which is delicious. You're going to braise it in Tecate, and it's gonna take a while to coax out every bit of flavor. Trust us when we say to get the twenty-four-pack. Making tamales is a true family affair, and this isn't a fast recipe. Put the beers on ice, have some snacks handy to keep the vibes chill, and by sundown you'll be feasting like a Mayan king.

2 lb (1 kg) oxtails, cut into 3-inch (7.5-cm) pieces

Kosher salt and freshly ground pepper

3 Tbsp extra-virgin olive oil

2 garlic cloves, crushed

1 can (12 fl oz/375 ml) Tecate or other Mexican lager

6 mixed dried chiles, such as ancho, árbol, and chipotle, stemmed

17 dried corn husks

2 cups (8 oz/250 g) masa harina, plus more if needed

1 cup (8 fl oz/250 ml) chicken stock, plus more if needed

1 tsp baking powder

2/3 cup (5½ oz/170 g) lard, melted and cooled slightly

½ lb (250 g) fresh goat cheese, crumbled

Season the oxtails with salt and pepper. In a Dutch oven or other large pot with a tight-fitting lid that just fits the oxtails, heat the olive oil over medium-high heat. Add the oxtails and sear on all sides, 5–10 minutes total. Add the garlic and cook for 1 minute, then add the beer and chiles. Bring to a boil, then reduce the heat to low and simmer until the oxtails are tender and falling off the bone, about 2 hours.

Meanwhile, put the corn husks in a large bowl and add hot water to submerge completely. Soak until the husks are soft and pliable, about 2 hours.

When the oxtails are ready, transfer them to a cutting board. When they are cool enough to handle, remove the meat from the bones and discard the bones, any cartilage, and connective tissue. Transfer the meat to a bowl and pour in just enough cooking liquid to barely moisten it. Taste and adjust the seasoning.

Transfer the chiles to a blender and purée with enough cooking liquid to make a smooth paste.

In a bowl, stir together the masa harina, stock, baking powder, 1½ teaspoons salt, and the lard. The mixture should feel like firm, wet sand. Adjust with more masa harina or stock if needed.

Drain the corn husks and pat dry. Tear 1–2 husks lengthwise into long, narrow strips for tying the tamales; you will need 15 strips. Set aside. Lay a husk on a flat work surface. Place a golf ball–size ball of dough in the center of the husk, smash it with your hand to form a rectangle, then spread it over the husk about ½ inch (12 mm) thick, leaving a 1-inch (2.5-cm) border uncovered on all sides. Put about 2 tablespoons cheese, ½ teaspoon chile purée, and 1–2 tablespoons oxtail meat in the center of the dough. Fold the corn husk over lengthwise, covering the filling with the dough. Fold the husk over one more time, then fold the bottom end of the husk up over the tamale and secure the end in place with a husk strip. Repeat to fill the remaining corn husks.

Place a steamer insert in the bottom of a large pot, add water to the pot to just below (but not touching) the base of the insert. Arrange the tamales, open side up, in the insert, and bring the water to a boil. Cover the pot and steam the tamales for 1–1½ hours, replenishing the water with hot water as needed. To check for doneness, pull out 1 tamale and try to unwrap it. If the husk comes away from the masa cleanly, the masa is firm, and the filling is warm through, it's ready. If not, continue cooking until done, checking every 15 minutes and replenishing the water as needed.

Transfer the tamales to a platter and let cool slightly before serving.

GUMBO
with crispy okra

We have never been to New Orleans. We have never trained under a Southern chef. We haven't even read a huge amount about Creole and Cajun cuisines. And we have never tasted your family's recipe for gumbo that has been passed down through ten generations. This is a new, reimagined version of gumbo with fried okra. We made it up. It's not authentic. Please put down your pitchforks and other murderous tools now.

1 lb (500 g) shrimp in the shell

5 Tbsp (3 fl oz/80 ml) extra-virgin olive oil

2 cups (16 fl oz/500 ml) beef stock

2 cups (10 oz/315 g) mixed finely diced celery, red bell pepper, and yellow onion, in equal parts

2 garlic cloves, minced

1 jalapeño chile, minced

2 Tbsp all-purpose flour, plus 1 cup (5 oz/155 g)

2 tsp Tabasco sauce

1 cup (4 oz/125 g) sliced okra

Kosher salt

1 lb (500 g) spicy chicken sausage (andouille style, if possible), sliced or crumbled

2 cups (12 oz/375 g) cooked wild rice, kept warm

Peel and devein the shrimp, reserving the shells. Refrigerate the shrimp until ready to cook.

In a saucepan, heat 1 tablespoon of the olive oil over high heat. Add the shrimp shells and cook, stirring, until browned, 3–4 minutes. Add the stock, reduce the heat to very low, and simmer gently for 30 minutes. Strain the stock and discard the shells.

In a large saucepan, heat 2 tablespoons of the olive oil over low heat. Add the celery, bell pepper, onion, garlic, and jalapeño and sauté until softened, about 10 minutes. Add the 2 tablespoons flour and cook, stirring constantly, for 5 minutes. Add the reserved stock and the Tabasco and simmer for 10 minutes. Remove from the heat and set aside.

Meanwhile, in a heavy frying pan, heat the remaining 2 tablespoons olive oil over high heat. Put the 1 cup (5 oz/155 g) flour in a bowl. Season the okra with salt and then dredge in the flour, shaking off the excess. Carefully add the okra to the pan and sauté until brown and crispy, about 3 minutes. Using a slotted spoon, transfer the okra to a paper towel–lined plate to drain, then season with salt.

In the same frying pan, cook the shrimp and sausage over medium heat until just cooked through, 5–6 minutes. Add the stock mixture and bring to a simmer.

Divide the wild rice evenly among individual bowls. Ladle the gumbo on top and garnish with the fried okra. Serve right away.

TV dinner CLASSICS

you're gonna eat in front of the TV,

SO IT MAY AS WELL BE DELICIOUS

Rabbit Potpie 50 • *Lamb Meat Loaf with Curried Potatoes* 52

Hangar Steak with Roasted Sunchoke Salad 53

Turkey Dinner 56 • *Crispy Fish with Salt & Vinegar Chips* 57

Popcorn Shrimp with Leek-Chile Butter 59

Pan-Seared Cod with Roasted Squash & Pancetta 62

FEATURING: GIN COCKTAILS 60

rabbit POTPIE

You could invite six friends over, make these potpies, and share. Or, you could lock your doors, call in to work to tell them you won't be coming in this week, cuddle up with *The West Wing*, and eat rabbit potpies as you watch people walking fast through hallways while talking even faster.

pastry dough

2½ cups (12½ oz/390 g) all-purpose flour

1 tsp kosher salt

2 Tbsp minced fresh rosemary

1 cup (8 oz/250 g) cold unsalted butter, cut into small pieces

¼ cup (2 fl oz/60 ml) ice water, plus more if needed

filling

2 Tbsp vegetable oil

1 rabbit, separated into the saddle, hind legs, and front legs

Kosher salt and freshly ground pepper

¼ cup (1¼ oz/40 g) all-purpose flour

½ cup (2½ oz/75 g) diced carrot

½ cup (2½ oz/75 g) diced yellow onion

½ cup (2½ oz/75 g) diced Yukon gold potato, blanched and cooled

1 cup (8 fl oz/250 ml) dry white wine

1 cup (8 fl oz/250 ml) chicken stock

½ cup (4 fl oz/125 ml) heavy cream

3 Tbsp cornstarch dissolved in ¼ cup (2 fl oz/60 ml) water

½ cup (2½ oz/75 g) shelled English peas, blanched

¼ cup (⅓ oz/10 g) chopped fresh tarragon

1 large egg beaten with 1 Tbsp water

In a food processor, combine the flour, salt, and rosemary. Pulse to combine. Add the butter and pulse until the butter chunks are pea size. Slowly add the ice water and pulse until the dough comes together. Squeeze the dough between your fingers; it should stay together rather than crumble apart; if it does crumble, add a little more water.

Turn the dough out onto a lightly floured work surface, knead the dough a few times until it comes together, then shape into a rectangle. Wrap with plastic wrap and refrigerate for at least 30 minutes. You can make the dough ahead of time and refrigerate it for up to 1 day or freeze it for up to 1 month. If the dough is frozen, let it thaw in the refrigerator for 1 day before using.

To make the filling, in a Dutch oven or other large, heavy-bottomed pot, heat the vegetable oil over medium heat. Season the rabbit with salt and pepper, then dredge in flour, shaking off the excess. Add the rabbit to the hot oil and cook, turning as needed to ensure even browning, until lightly browned, about 5 minutes. Transfer the rabbit to a plate and reserve. Add the carrot, onion, and potato to the pot and cook, stirring occasionally, until slightly softened and caramelized, about 5 minutes. Return the rabbit pieces to the pot, add the wine, stock, and cream, and bring to a simmer. Cover and cook until the rabbit pieces are tender, transferring them to a cutting board as they are done. The loin will cook in about 10 minutes and the legs may take up to 30 minutes.

Preheat the oven to 350°F (180°C).

When the rabbit is cool enough to handle, remove the meat from the bones, discarding the bones. Chop the meat into bite-size pieces and return it to the cooking liquid. Place the pot over medium heat and reheat the rabbit mixture. Stir in the cornstarch mixture, peas, and tarragon. Taste and adjust the seasoning.

Have ready six 4-inch (10-cm) ramekins. On a lightly floured work surface, roll out the dough about ¼ inch (6 mm) thick. Using a knife and a template, cut out 6 rounds that are slightly wider than the ramekins. Fill the ramekins with the rabbit mixture to within ½ inch (12 mm) of the rim. Place a dough round over each ramekin and crimp the edges with a fork. Brush the tops with the egg wash and cut a vent in the top. Place the ramekins on a rimmed baking sheet.

Bake the potpies until the crust is golden brown and the filling is bubbly, about 25 minutes. Let cool slightly before serving.

LAMB MEAT LOAF
with curried potatoes

Just like Tony Danza, meat loaf is back in the spotlight and cooler than ever. But like any recipe, this is just a suggested starting place for a great meat loaf. Because really . . . *Who's the Boss?* You are. Don't let a career-ending sports injury or being a single mother stop you. We think this meat loaf is just the thing you need to help you pursue "a brand new life around the bend."

lamb meat loaf

2 Tbsp extra-virgin olive oil

1 cup (5 oz/155 g) *each* finely diced carrot, celery, and yellow onion

1 lb (500 g) ground lamb

2 Tbsp tomato paste

1 garlic clove, minced

¼ cup (2 oz/60 g) whole-milk Greek yogurt

1 large egg, beaten

3 Tbsp panko bread crumbs

2 Tbsp *sambal olek* (Asian chile paste)

1½ tsp kosher salt

1 tsp firmly packed light brown sugar

¼ tsp *each* hot paprika and ground coriander

curried potatoes

1½ lb (750 g) small Yukon gold potatoes

1 Tbsp kosher salt

4 Tbsp (2 oz/60 g) unsalted butter

¼ cup (2 oz/60 g) whole-milk Greek yogurt

¼ cup (2 fl oz/60 ml) whole milk, plus more if needed

3 Tbsp curry powder

1 cup (5 oz/155 g) shelled English peas

1 Fresno chile, seeded and thinly sliced

¼ cup (⅓ oz/10 g) *each* chopped fresh mint leaves and cilantro leaves and stems

Juice of 2 limes

To make the meat loaf, in a sauté pan, heat the olive oil over low heat. Add the carrot, celery, and onion and cook, stirring occasionally, until very soft and slightly caramelized, about 45 minutes. Let cool.

Preheat the oven to 375°F (190°C).

In a large bowl, combine the lamb, tomato paste, garlic, yogurt, egg, panko, sambal olek, salt, brown sugar, paprika, coriander, and the carrot mixture. Mix gently with your hands just until combined; you don't want to overwork the meat. Transfer to a 9-by-5-inch (23-by-13-cm) loaf pan. Bake the meat loaf until it is browned and just cooked through, about 40 minutes. Let cool slightly.

Meanwhile, to make the potatoes, put them in a large saucepan and add water to cover. Bring to a boil over high heat, then stir in the salt. Reduce the heat to medium and cook until tender, about 20 minutes. Drain the potatoes.

In the same pan, combine the butter, yogurt, milk, curry powder, peas, chile, mint, cilantro, and lime juice. Place the pan over medium heat and cook, stirring, until a saucy consistency is reached, 3–4 minutes; add more milk if needed. Return the potatoes to the pan and stir to coat with the sauce.

Cut the meat loaf into slices and serve with the curried potatoes.

HANGAR STEAK
with roasted sunchoke salad

One "Ga Ga Ga Ga!" from Kramer, one "Get Out!" from Elaine, one "Jerry!" from George, or one "Newman!" from Jerry are all you need from *Seinfeld* to be satisfied. A hangar steak is like the perfect catchphrase. Even if it's slightly overdone, it's always completely satisfying. Avoid the Soup Nazi. Don't eat an éclair out of the trash. Skip meeting the gang for stale coffee and soft fries at The Restaurant. Fire up the Walkman and eat some steak in bed.

4 garlic cloves, minced

Leaves from 1 fresh rosemary sprig

Leaves from 2 fresh thyme sprigs

1 cup (8 fl oz/250 ml) extra-virgin olive oil, plus 2 Tbsp

Kosher salt and freshly ground pepper

4 hangar steaks, each about 7 oz (220 g)

2 cups (16 fl oz/500 ml) whole milk

2 large celery roots, about 2 lb (1 kg) total weight, peeled and cubed

1 large russet potato, peeled and cubed

3 shallots, coarsely chopped

3 Tbsp unsalted butter

1 lb (500 g) sunchokes, unpeeled and roughly chopped into 1-inch (2.5-cm) pieces

1/2 bunch green onions, white and tender green parts only, cut into 1/2-inch (12-mm) batons

Leaves from 1 bunch fresh flat-leaf parsley

Sea salt

In a glass baking dish, stir together the garlic, rosemary, thyme, 1 cup (8 fl oz/250 ml) olive oil, and 1 tablespoon kosher salt. Add the steaks and turn to coat with the marinade. Cover and refrigerate for at least 2 hours but preferably overnight.

Preheat the oven to 375°F (190°C).

In a stockpot, combine the milk, 2 cups (16 fl oz/500 ml) water, and 1 teaspoon kosher salt and bring to a boil over high heat. Add the celery roots, potato, and shallots, reduce the heat to medium-low, and simmer until the vegetables are tender, about 30 minutes.

Using a slotted spoon, transfer the celery roots, potato, and shallots to a blender, reserving the cooking liquid. With the blender on low speed, slowly add the liquid, 1 tablespoon at a time, until the mixture forms a smooth purée. Add the butter and blend until combined. The purée should be thick but still pourable. Transfer the purée to a bowl. Taste and adjust the seasoning. Cover to keep warm.

While the celery roots, potato, and shallots are cooking, in a bowl, toss the sunchokes with the 2 tablespoons olive oil and sprinkle with kosher salt and pepper. Transfer to a rimmed baking sheet and roast until golden brown, 20–25 minutes. Remove the sunchokes from the oven and toss with the green onions and parsley. Sprinkle with sea salt and keep warm.

About 15 minutes before the purée and sunchokes are ready, build a hot fire in a charcoal grill or preheat a gas grill to high. Using a grill brush, scrape the heated grill rack clean. Alternatively, heat a large cast-iron frying pan on the stove top over high heat.

Place the steaks on the grill or in the frying pan and cook, turning once, for about 3 minutes on each side for rare, 4 minutes for medium-rare, and 6 minutes for well-done. Transfer the steaks to a cutting board and let rest for 5 minutes.

To serve, cut the steaks against the grain into thin slices. Spoon the celery root purée onto individual plates, arrange the steaks on the purée, and top with the sunchoke salad.

TURKEY
dinner

If you're watching various men fall from grace—be they going mad, breaking bad, or turning to a life of anarchy—don't settle for some waxy, dry, microwavable turkey dinner. This massive drumstick dish is the perfect pairing for an evening of absurdity, excess, and machismo.

brine
1 cup (8 oz/250 g) kosher salt

1 cup (8 oz/250 g) sugar

4 árbol chiles

1 bay leaf

1 fresh thyme sprig

2 Tbsp peppercorns

1 lemon, halved

2 turkey drumsticks, about 1½ lb (750 g) total weight

spice rub
¼ cup (1 oz/30 g) hot paprika

2 Tbsp sweet paprika

2 tsp freshly ground pepper

2 tsp garlic powder

2 tsp kosher salt

½ tsp sugar

1 cup (8 fl oz/250 ml) chicken stock

½ cup (2½ oz/75 g) chopped carrots

stuffing
4 Tbsp (2 oz/60 g) unsalted butter

3 large carrots, peeled and roughly cut into ½-inch (12-mm) pieces

Heart from 1 bunch celery, roughly cut into ½-inch (12-mm) pieces

1 large white onion, diced

Leaves from 2 fresh rosemary sprigs

Leaves from 3 fresh thyme sprigs

1 loaf (1 lb/500 g) challah, torn into chunks

1 cup (8 fl oz/250 ml) chicken stock, plus more as needed

To make the brine, in a large pot, combine 8 quarts (8 l) water, the salt, sugar, chiles, bay leaf, thyme, peppercorns, and lemon and bring to a boil over high heat, stirring to dissolve the salt and sugar. Remove from the heat and let cool completely.

Add the turkey drumsticks to the brine, making sure they are submerged. To weight them down, set a plate with a can on top. Cover with plastic wrap and refrigerate for 24 hours.

Preheat the oven to 375°F (190°C). Remove the drumsticks from the brine and pat dry with paper towels. Discard the brine.

To make the spice rub, in a small bowl, stir together the hot paprika, sweet paprika, pepper, garlic powder, salt, and sugar. Coat the turkey drumsticks all over with the spice rub.

Place the drumsticks on a rimmed baking sheet and roast until browned and the fat starts to render out slightly, about 20 minutes. Reduce the oven temperature to 300°F (150°C) and add the stock and the chopped carrots to the pan. Continue roasting until the turkey drumsticks are tender and the meat is nearly falling off the bone, about 1 hour longer.

To make the stuffing, in a Dutch oven or other large, heavy-bottomed pot, melt the butter over medium-low heat. Add the carrots, celery, onion, rosemary, and thyme and cook, stirring occasionally, until golden brown, about 10 minutes. Add the challah, stir well, and cook until some of the bread is toasted, about 4 minutes. Add the stock and simmer until the bread has absorbed all of the liquid, about 10 minutes. Continue cooking until some of the bits of bread are crispy again, about 3 minutes longer. For softer stuffing, add more stock, ¼ cup (2 fl oz/60 ml) at a time, until the desired consistency.

Serve the drumsticks topped with the pan drippings and with the stuffing alongside.

CRISPY FISH
with salt & vinegar chips

America likes to take what works abroad, repackage it slightly, and call it our own. Steve Carell is arguably as strong as Ricky Gervais in *The Office*, and the US version of *House of Cards* has swept the nation, so there's been some success in copying what the British have done. But for some reason, fish and chips has never had the full-on cultural takeover it deserves. Well, get ready, because with this recipe, fish and chips is having its moment.

1 large baguette, quartered crosswise and halved lengthwise to make 4 sandwiches

crab dip
6 oz (185 g) crabmeat, picked over for cartilage and shell fragments

½ cup (4 fl oz/125 ml) mayonnaise

1 tsp fresh lemon juice

1 tsp Dijon mustard

1 Tbsp chopped fresh dill

1 Tbsp thinly sliced fresh chives

chips
4 cups (32 fl oz/1 l) vegetable oil

1 russet potato

2 Tbsp malt vinegar powder

1 tsp sea salt

fish
2½ cups (12½ oz/390 g) all-purpose flour

1 bottle (12 fl oz/375 ml) dark beer

1 tsp baking powder

1 large egg

2 Tbsp ancho chile powder

1 tsp kosher salt

1 tsp freshly ground pepper

4 hake fillets, each about ¼ lb (125 g)

Preheat the oven to 400°F (200°C). Place the bread pieces, cut side up, on a baking sheet and toast until golden, 5–7 minutes.

To make the crab dip, in a bowl, stir together the crabmeat, mayonnaise, lemon juice, mustard, dill, and chives. Set aside.

To make the chips, in a small, deep pot, heat the vegetable oil over medium heat to 325°F (165°C). Line a baking sheet with paper towels. Using a mandoline, slice the potato as thinly as possible, about half the thickness of a credit card.

Add half of the potato slices to the hot oil and fry until golden brown, about 5 minutes. Using a slotted spoon, transfer to a large bowl and immediately toss with half each of the malt vinegar powder and sea salt. Transfer to the prepared baking sheet to dry. Repeat with the remaining potato slices, sea salt, and vinegar powder.

Increase the oil temperature to 350°F (180°C). To make the fish, in a bowl, whisk together 2 cups (10 oz/315 g) of the flour, the beer, baking powder, egg, and chile powder to make a batter. Put the remaining ½ cup (2½ oz/75 g) flour in a small bowl and add the kosher salt and pepper.

Working with 1 hake fillet at a time, dredge the fish in the seasoned flour, shaking off the excess, then place in the batter. Lift out the fish, allowing some of the excess batter to drip off. Working in batches to avoid crowding, gently add the fish to the hot oil and fry until golden brown, 5–6 minutes. Using tongs, transfer to paper towels to drain.

To assemble each sandwich, place a piece of fish on the bottom piece of a baguette section. Top with one-fourth of the crab dip, then close the sandwich with the top piece of baguette. Serve right away with a side of chips.

POPCORN SHRIMP
with leek-chile butter

The Santa Monica pier holds the world's foremost shrimp mecca, Bubba Gump Shrimp. Named after one of the country's most famous citizens (himself an international Ping-Pong sensation, college football star, war hero, and, of course, in a later part of his life, a shrimping magnate), this restaurant has enticed diners from around the world to try the countless varieties of shrimp. And since the documentary of his life, *Forrest Gump*, is on TBS just about every five minutes, this is the perfect pairing when watching the true story of one of the nation's greats.

leek-chile butter

6-8 medium leeks, white and pale green parts only, cut into rounds

1 Tbsp extra-virgin olive oil

1 cup (8 oz/250 g) unsalted butter, melted and cooled to room temperature

1 tsp sea salt

1 tsp red pepper flakes

4 large eggs

¼ cup (2 fl oz/60 ml) buttermilk

1 tsp cayenne pepper

1 tsp ancho chile powder

1 tsp garlic powder

1 tsp freshly ground black pepper

½ tsp kosher salt

1 cup (5 oz/155 g) all-purpose flour

3-4 cups (4½-6 oz/140-185 g) panko bread crumbs

½ lb (250 g) shrimp, peeled and deveined

6 cups (48 fl oz/1.5 l) vegetable oil

Lemon wedges for serving

To make the leek-chile butter, preheat the oven to 350°F (180°C).

In a bowl, toss the leeks with the olive oil. Spread in a single layer on a baking sheet. Roast until golden brown and beginning to crisp, about 20 minutes. Let cool completely, then chop coarsely.

Put the butter in a bowl and fold in the leeks, sea salt, and red pepper flakes. Set aside.

Line a baking sheet with parchment paper. Line a second baking sheet with paper towels. In a bowl, whisk the eggs until well blended, then whisk in the buttermilk, cayenne, chile powder, garlic powder, black pepper, and kosher salt. Put the flour and panko into separate bowls.

Dredge the shrimp in the flour, shaking off the excess, then place the shrimp in the egg mixture and stir gently with your hands to coat the shrimp. Remove the shrimp from the egg mixture, letting the excess drip off, then coat the shrimp with the panko, again shaking off the excess. Place on the parchment-lined baking sheet.

In a large pot, heat the vegetable oil over high heat to 350°F (180°C).

Working in batches to avoid crowding, use a slotted spoon or a metal sieve to lower the shrimp into the hot oil. Fry until golden brown, about 3 minutes. Using the slotted spoon, transfer the shrimp to the towel-lined baking sheet to drain.

Serve the shrimp right away with lemon wedges and the leek-chile butter.

= GIN =

perhaps more than any other liquid

IS BUILT FOR COCKTAILS.

UNLIKE WHISKEY, TEQUILA, OR VODKA,

YOU DON'T DRINK SHOTS OF GIN.

If you order gin shots at a bar, the bartender may decline to serve you, because that's something a very, very sad alcoholic would do. And you're a functional social drinker with your life completely under control and your five-year plan unfolding just as you'd imagined. The herbaceous qualities of many gins make it an ideal starting point for cocktails that have fruit-flavored elements, which is what we've done here with our updates on three slightly obscure, yet classic gin drinks. This isn't the type of situation in the cookbook where we'd say, "If you aren't a fan of gin, no worries! Just sub in vodka or whiskey!" These cocktails don't work like that. They are written for gin and built for sipping. The Tuxedo and Reviver (and the fizz minus the egg) are definitely ideal for large batching for a party (or a party of one that hates making drinks one at a time). And you know

WHAT GOES PERFECTLY WITH THAT FIVE-YEAR PLAN?

FIVE OF THESE COCKTAILS.

THE BLACK TUXEDO

2 fl oz (60 ml) Plymouth gin

¾ fl oz (20 ml) Dolin dry vermouth

1 fl oz (30 ml) Cynar

2 dashes orange bitters

1 dash fresh lemon juice

Ice

serves 1

This is a take on the Tuxedo No. 2, one of Eli's favorite drinks, prepared here with Cynar. An Italian bitter liqueur, Cynar is made with artichokes and provides a satisfying botanical bitterness that pairs brilliantly with gin. It's the ideal aperitif and can also be sipped all the way through the meal.

Combine the gin, vermouth, Cynar, bitters, and lemon juice in a mixing glass with ice. Stir for 15 seconds, then strain into a chilled martini glass and serve.

LEMON-LIME FIZZ

3 fl oz (90 ml) 7UP

2 fl oz (60 ml) gin

1 large egg white

3 ice cubes

1 lemon wedge

1 lime wedge

serves 1

This drink takes the best parts of a Tom Collins and of a gin fizz and joins them together in holy boozy matrimony. It pairs perfectly with the Preserved Lemon Key Lime Pie on page 140.

Pour the 7UP into a chilled tumbler. Combine the gin, egg white, and ice cubes in a cocktail shaker. Cover and shake for 10 seconds, then strain into the tumbler. Garnish with the lemon and lime wedges and serve.

THE WALKING DEAD REVIVER

1 fl oz (30 ml) gin

1 fl oz (30 ml) Lillet Blanc

1 fl oz (30 ml) Pernod

½ fl oz (15 ml) fresh lime juice

4 ice cubes

5 drops grenadine

1 drop absinthe

serves 1

A modern take on the Corpse Reviver, this drink is sure to bring anyone in a zombielike state from the night before back into real life. It's got a kick from the absinthe that's a real shot to the head.

Combine the gin, Lillet, Pernod, lime juice, and ice cubes in a cocktail shaker. Cover and shake for 15 seconds, then strain into a chilled cocktail glass. Add the grenadine and then the absinthe and serve.

PAN-SEARED COD
with roasted squash & pancetta

Like Balki Bartokomous and his cuzin Larry, this surf-'n'-turf pairing is quite the unlikely combo. Seared cod with crispy pancetta takes the place of the traditional overcooked steak and rubbery lobster. Wondra is a marvel of the modern world: a fine-grain flour that doesn't clump, so it's great for coating delicate-skin fish with a thin layer to prevent sticking in the pan. Don't let you and your home kitchen become perfect strangers. Don't be afraid to start cooking. It's your life, it's your dream. And nothin' is gonna stop you now.

¾ lb (375 g) small yellow pattypan squashes, halved

4 Tbsp (2 fl oz/60 ml) extra-virgin olive oil

Kosher salt and freshly ground black pepper

6 oz (185 g) pancetta, diced

2 skin-on cod fillets, each about 6 oz (185 g)

Wondra flour for coating

1 Tbsp unsalted butter

¼ cup (¼ oz/7 g) fresh flat-leaf parsley leaves

2 Tbsp thinly sliced chives

1 tsp red pepper flakes

Grated zest and juice of 1 lemon

Preheat the oven to 375°F (190°C).

In a bowl, toss the squash with 2 tablespoons of the olive oil and sprinkle with salt and black pepper. Spread in a single layer on a rimmed baking sheet and roast until golden brown, 20–25 minutes.

Meanwhile, in a nonstick frying pan, cook the pancetta over medium heat until crispy, 4–7 minutes. Remove the pan from the heat and cover to keep warm.

Pat the cod dry with paper towels. Sprinkle generously with salt and then lightly coat with flour, shaking off the excess.

In another nonstick frying pan, heat the remaining 2 tablespoons olive oil over medium heat. When the oil is hot, add the fish, skin side down, and cook for about 3 minutes. Flip the fish and cook for about 2 minutes, then add the butter to the pan and cook the fish until a cake tester inserted into the center is very warm but not hot to the touch, about 30 seconds longer. Transfer the fish to a paper towel–lined plate to drain.

Transfer the squash to a bowl. Add the pancetta, parsley, chives, red pepper flakes, lemon zest, and lemon juice and toss to combine. Taste and adjust the seasoning.

Spoon the squash mixture onto individual plates and top with the fish. Serve right away.

4

les
CLASSIQUES

recipes from the French canon that are

REALLY GOOD & NOT THAT HARD

TOMATO TART
with arugula salad

This is the kind of dish inspired by great tomatoes during the peak of summer.
For the best flavor and color, go to your local farmers' market and buy the freshest,
most spectacular heirloom tomatoes you can find. Come on, just look at that picture . . .

pastry dough

2½ cups (12½ oz/390 g) all-purpose flour

1 tsp kosher salt

½ tsp sugar

1 cup (8 oz/250 g) cold unsalted butter,
cut into small pieces

¼ cup (2 fl oz/60 ml) ice water,
plus more if needed

tomato tart

3 or 4 large heirloom tomatoes,
sliced ¼ inch (6 mm) thick

Kosher salt and freshly ground pepper

2 tablespoons extra-virgin olive oil

2½ oz (75 g) fresh goat cheese,
at room temperature

1½ cups (12 fl oz/380 ml) heavy cream

1 tsp chopped fresh thyme

salad

¼ cup (2 oz/60 g) oil-packed sun-dried
tomatoes, drained

¼ cup (2 fl oz/60 ml) balsamic vinegar

½ cup (4 fl oz/125 ml) extra-virgin olive oil

1 tsp kosher salt

¼ tsp freshly ground pepper

1 cup (6 oz/185 g) cherry or grape tomatoes,
halved and/or quartered, or 1 heirloom
tomato, cut into ½-inch (12-mm) pieces

2 cups (2 oz/60 g) baby arugula

In a food processor, combine the flour, salt, and sugar and pulse to combine. Add the butter and pulse until the butter chunks are pea size. Slowly add the ice water and pulse until the dough comes together. Squeeze the dough between your fingers; it should stay together rather than crumble apart. If it does crumble, add a little more water.

Turn the dough out onto a lightly floured work surface, knead the dough a few times until it comes together, then shape it into a rectangle. Wrap with plastic wrap and refrigerate for at least 30 minutes. You can make the dough ahead of time and refrigerate it for up to 3 days or freeze it for up to 1 month. If the dough is frozen, let it thaw in the refrigerator for 1 day before using.

On a lightly floured work surface, roll out the dough into a rectangle about ¼ inch (6 mm) thick and slightly larger than a rimmed baking sheet. Fold the dough into quarters, transfer it to the baking sheet, unfold it, and press it into the corners of the pan. Crimp edges, if desired, and refrigerate for at least 30 minutes before using.

Preheat the oven to 425°F (220°C). Line a baking sheet with parchment paper.

To make the tart, place the tomato slices in a single layer on the prepared baking sheet. Sprinkle with salt and drizzle with the olive oil. Roast until just browned on the edges, 15–20 minutes. Transfer the tomatoes to the refrigerator to cool. Reduce the oven temperature to 350°F (180°C).

Remove the dough-lined pan from the refrigerator. In a small bowl, stir together the goat cheese, cream, and a pinch each of salt and pepper. Spread the cheese mixture evenly over the dough, extending it to the edges. Arrange the cooled tomatoes on top, spacing them evenly, and sprinkle with the thyme. Bake until the crust is golden brown, 25–30 minutes.

Meanwhile, make the salad: In a food processor or blender, combine the sun-dried tomatoes, vinegar, olive oil, salt, pepper, and 2 tablespoons water and purée until mostly smooth. In a bowl, toss the cherry tomatoes and arugula with the vinaigrette to taste.

Garnish the hot tart with the salad, cut the tart into pieces, and serve right away.

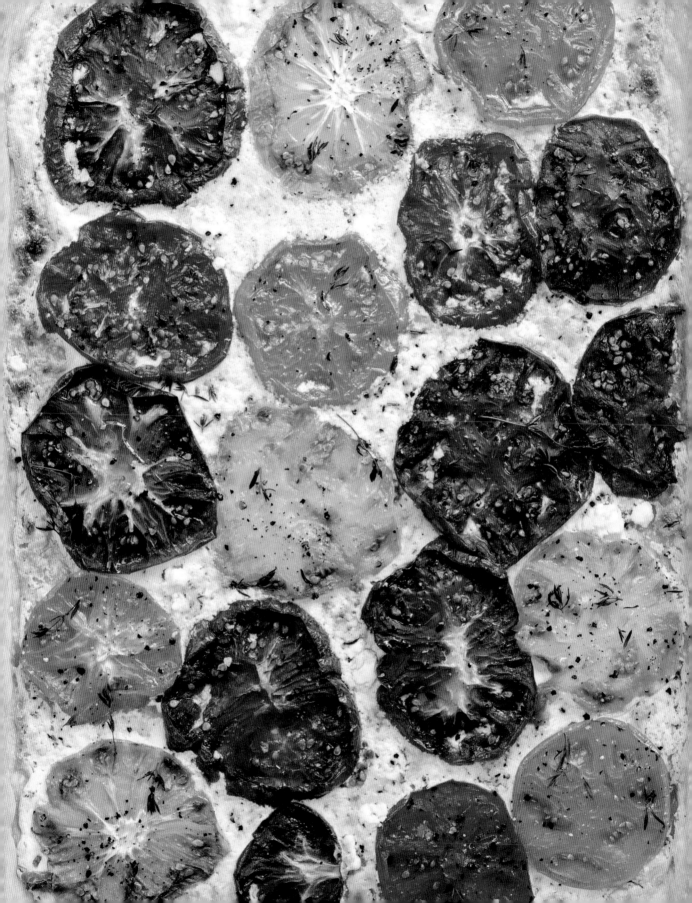

CHICKEN LIVER MOUSSE
with blackberries & toast

As a couple of Jews, we have a very specific childhood memory of chicken liver as something involving white onions, lots of hard-boiled eggs, a lack of seasoning, and an end product no one really loved. But as we became better chefs, we learned about other ways to prepare chicken liver that are sensational. This new take is silky smooth, spreadable, and includes a touch of sweetness. It's definitely not the chopped liver we grew up with.

1 cup (4 oz/125 g) blackberries

½ cup (4 oz/125 g) sugar

Kosher salt and freshly ground pepper

½ lb (250 g) bacon, cut into 1-inch (2.5-cm) pieces

¾ lb (375 g) fresh chicken livers, dried very well with paper towels

¼ lb (125 g) shallots, minced

1 garlic clove, minced

½ cup (4 fl oz/125 ml) Moscato or other semisweet white wine

6 Tbsp (3 oz/90 g) unsalted butter, at room temperature

Brioche slices, toasted, for serving

In a small bowl, toss together the blackberries, sugar, and a pinch of salt. Set aside.

In a frying pan, cook the bacon over medium heat until crispy, about 5 minutes. Transfer to paper towels to drain. Keep half of the fat in the pan, and reserve the remainder for another use.

Place the pan over high heat. Season the chicken livers generously with salt. Working in batches if needed to avoid crowding, add the livers and sear, turning once, until they are browned but just warmed through, 1–2 minutes on each side. Transfer to a plate in a single layer and place in the freezer or refrigerator until cold but not frozen.

Reduce the heat to medium, add the shallots and garlic, and sauté until softened, 2–3 minutes. Add the wine and deglaze the pan, scraping up any browned bits from the bottom, then simmer for 2 minutes. Transfer to a heatproof bowl and let cool completely in the refrigerator.

In a food processor or blender, combine the chicken livers, bacon, butter, shallot mixture, 1 teaspoon salt, and ½ teaspoon pepper and purée until smooth. Taste and adjust the seasoning.

To serve, spread the brioche toast with the mousse and garnish with the macerated blackberries.

salade
NIÇOISE

Salade Niçoise is like the Mona Lisa of salads, and that's why we picked it for this chapter.
Enigmatic, whimsical, with just a hint of mystery. There's something about the way the ingredients combine
differently with each bite that makes you keep coming back for more. It's simple on the surface,
yet it's more complex each time you try it. So delicious, it will put a smile on your face. Or is it a smile?

dressing

4 hard-boiled eggs, peeled and chopped

5 tsp spicy Dijon mustard

1 Tbsp sherry vinegar

1/2 cup (2 1/2 oz/75 g) finely diced cornichons

1/4 cup (2 oz/60 g) capers

1/2 cup (4 fl oz/125 ml) extra-virgin olive oil

2 Tbsp chopped fresh tarragon

1 oz (30 g) white anchovy fillets, minced

1/2 lb (250 g) Yukon gold potatoes, boiled
until fork-tender, cooled, and quartered

1/2 lb (250 g) red potatoes, boiled until
fork-tender, cooled, and quartered

1/2 lb (250 g) green beans, trimmed,
blanched, and cooled in an ice bath

1 pint (12 oz/375 g) cherry tomatoes, halved

1/2 bunch radishes, very thinly sliced

2 Persian cucumbers, thinly sliced

1/2 cup (2 oz/60 g) julienned red onion

1/2 cup (2 1/2 oz/75 g) small black olives,
preferably Niçoise

1 can (4 oz/125 g) high-quality tuna
(humanely and sustainably caught),
drained and flaked

6 oz (185 g) small golden beets, boiled until
fork-tender, peeled, and quartered

2 hard-boiled eggs, peeled and halved
lengthwise (optional)

To make the dressing, in a bowl, stir together the eggs, mustard, and vinegar until well combined. Stir in the cornichons and capers. While stirring, slowly add the oil until blended, then fold in the tarragon and anchovies. The dressing should be thick but still pourable (like ranch dressing); if necessary, stir in warm water, 1 tablespoon at a time, until it reaches the desired consistency.

In a large bowl, stir and toss together the potatoes, green beans, tomatoes, radishes, cucumbers, onion, olives, and tuna. Transfer to a serving dish and garnish with the beets and eggs, if desired. Serve the dressing on the side.

asparagus & goat cheese POPOVERS

We were trying to come up with a soufflé recipe to go along with the old-school French theme of this chapter. What we soon realized was that we don't like soufflés, and we also didn't think anyone would ever make one. Popovers, on the other hand, are easy to make and everyone likes them. And we've made them a bunch of times. So, behold, our recipe for an asparagus souf . . . we mean popovers.

Olive oil spray

1 large egg

1 cup (8 fl oz/250 ml) whole milk

1 Tbsp unsalted butter, melted and cooled slightly

1/2 tsp firmly packed light brown sugar

1/2 tsp kosher salt

1/2 cup (2 1/2 oz/75 g) thinly sliced asparagus

2 Tbsp fresh goat cheese, crumbled

Scant 1 cup (5 oz/155 g) all-purpose flour

1 Tbsp whole-wheat flour

Preheat the oven to 425°F (220°C). Spray a 12-cup standard muffin pan with olive oil spray.

In a bowl, whisk together the egg, milk, butter, brown sugar, and salt. Fold in the asparagus and goat cheese. Gradually stir in the flours until the batter is smooth. Spoon into the prepared muffin cups, filling each cup about half full.

Bake for 10 minutes, then reduce the oven temperature to 350°F (180°C). Continue baking for about 15 minutes longer, without opening the oven door. To check if the popovers are fully cooked (no wet batter), tear one open. If it isn't ready, continue baking the popovers for about 5 minutes longer. Remove the popovers from the oven and eat right away.

SUMMER VEGETABLE
provençal

We smashed these two recipes together like 20th Century Fox smashed together *Alien* and *Predator* (but better). Our version takes all of the bright and bracing flavors of ratatouille and mixes them with the crispy, cheesy goodness of tomatoes Provençal. The result is a combo that is out-of-this-world delicious. Will we release a sequel? Only time will tell.

1 large heirloom tomato

2 zucchini

2 yellow squashes

1 Italian eggplant

3 garlic cloves

¼ cup (2 fl oz/60 ml) extra-virgin olive oil

Kosher salt

1 cup (1½ oz/45 g) panko bread crumbs

1 cup (4 oz/125 g) grated Parmesan cheese

1 Tbsp fresh thyme leaves

Preheat the oven to 450°F (230°C).

Cut the tomato, zucchini, yellow squashes, and eggplant into 2-inch (5-cm) pieces. You should have enough vegetables to cover a rimmed baking sheet in a thin layer. Put the vegetables and garlic cloves in a large bowl, add the olive oil and a generous pinch of salt, and toss to coat the vegetables evenly. Spread the vegetables in a single layer on a rimmed baking sheet.

Roast the vegetables until they are tender and crispy on the edges, about 40 minutes.

Meanwhile, in a small bowl, toss together the panko and cheese. When the vegetables are almost done, sprinkle them with the panko mixture and the thyme. Continue roasting until the bread crumbs are golden, about 10 minutes longer.

Break apart the sheet of vegetables and serve right away.

We consider ourselves connoisseurs of

THE ART OF CLASSIC PAIRINGS.

Lay down some plastic over the bearskin rug. Light one hundred candles to set the mood. A big vessel of steamy bubbling goodness is only moments away from flirtatiously caressing your lips. The windows are frosted over, the fire is crackling, you've got slippers and your favorite turtleneck on,

&

Barry White is telling you he just can't get enough. And you know what turtlenecks and Barry White pair with perfectly? A bottle of red decanted (so it can breathe) and small cauldrons filled with delicious, rich, piping-hot dippable sauces.

YOU READ THAT CORRECTLY. TAKE A BIG CHILL PILL.

WE'RE BRINGING FONDUE BACK.

Are you getting those hints of barnyard on the nose of that wine? Ohhhhh yeah. Dirty wine. Earthy funk. Nasty grapes. We assure you that a three-cheese fondue with pears simmering alongside a chocolate fondue with chunks of pound cake is what will get the temperature rising tonight. Or perhaps you're in the mood to get the blood flowing with a spicy, sticky, sweet Asian fondue with crisp wontons for dipping. Either way, fondue is the perfect aphrodisiac for a night of classic lovemaking. We're bringing it all back. Lovemaking, fondue, turtlenecks. Bearskin rugs. Sunken sofas. Barry White. Everything old is new again. But better. And hotter. And sweeter and stickier. Get ready to dip in.

CREAMY THREE-CHEESE FONDUE

1 cup (8 fl oz/250 ml) dry white wine

1 Tbsp unsalted butter

1 Tbsp all-purpose flour

7 oz (220 g) Gruyère cheese, cubed

7 oz (220 g) white Cheddar cheese, cubed

7 oz (220 g) Jarslberg cheese, cubed

Pear slices, apple slices, or toast points for serving

serves 2–4

The silky luxury of multiple cheeses intertwined in a rich embrace is an undeniable love potion. Close your eyes, inhale the aroma, and let your body take you where it's gonna go.

In a small saucepan, bring the wine to a boil over high heat.

Meanwhile, in a saucepan, melt the butter over medium heat, add the flour, and whisk to combine. Cook, whisking constantly to prevent scorching, for 3 minutes.

While whisking constantly, slowly pour the boiling wine into the flour mixture. When the wine is fully incorporated, slowly add the cheeses, a few cubes at a time, whisking after each addition until fully melted before adding more. Continue in this manner until all of the cheese is melted and the mixture is smooth.

Transfer the fondue to a fondue pot set over a low flame. Serve with pear slices for dipping.

SPICY ASIAN FONDUE

⅓ cup (3 oz/90 g) sugar

½ cup (4 fl oz/125 ml) rice wine vinegar

Cloves from ½ head garlic, minced

2 oz (60 g) fresh ginger, peeled and minced

2 tsp red pepper flakes

½ tsp kosher salt

1 cup (8 oz/250 g) tomato ketchup

1 Tbsp cornstarch, dissolved in ¼ cup (2 fl oz/60 ml) water

Deep-fried wontons and beans for serving

serves 2–4

The smoke from the incense and the flickering candlelight shrouds your guests' faces in sexy mystery. The anonymity makes for impassioned dipping. Breathe in the vapor of thousands of years of mystical Asian eroticism. Dip. Taste. Consume and be consumed.

In a saucepan, combine the sugar, vinegar, garlic, ginger, red pepper flakes, salt, and ½ cup (4 fl oz/125 ml) water and bring to a boil over high heat. Reduce the heat to medium-low so the mixture simmers. Add the ketchup and stir to mix well. Raise the heat to high and bring the mixture to a simmer. Whisk the cornstarch mixture briefly to recombine, then whisk it into the ketchup mixture until the mixture thickens.

Transfer the fondue to a fondue pot set over a low flame. Serve with crispy wontons for dipping.

CHOCOLATE-CARDAMARO FONDUE

½ lb (250 g) bittersweet chocolate

2 Tbsp Cardamaro (cardoon-flavored digestif) or port

1 cup (8 fl oz/250 ml) heavy cream

1 Tbsp unsalted butter, at room temperature

2 Tbsp finely chopped toasted walnuts (optional)

Pound cake, brownies, strawberries, and/or maraschino cherries for serving

serves 2–4

The sofa has been vacuumed and the pillows have been plumped. Decant the Merlot. That wine isn't breathing, baby, it's panting. Things are about to get provocative in a libidinous, chocolatey way. Come by for a dip. Clothing optional.

In the top pan of a double boiler, melt the chocolate over (but not touching) simmering water, stirring occasionally until smooth. Add the Cardamaro and cook, stirring gently, for 2 minutes. Remove from the heat and stir in the cream and butter.

Transfer the fondue to a fondue pot set over a low flame. Sprinkle with the walnuts, if desired. Serve with pound cake for dipping.

roasted stuffed
TROUT

Wrapping a fish in parchment paper for cooking is a lost art. The technique concentrates the flavors by steaming the fish in its own juices. It's a great move to have in your cooking arsenal. We think it went out of style sometime during the late 1980s or early 1990s when everyone started cutting foods into perfect circles and using squeeze bottles to dot sauces onto plates. It's quite hard to make a whole fish wrapped in paper look modernist. Instead, it just looks real and appetizing and tasty, which is what food should actually be about.

12 cherry tomatoes, halved

1 red onion, cut into ½-inch (12-mm) pieces

1 fennel bulb, trimmed, cored, and thinly sliced

1 lemon, cut into slices ¼ inch (6 mm) thick, plus lemon wedges for serving

Up to ¼ cup (2 fl oz/60 ml) extra-virgin olive oil

Kosher salt and freshly ground pepper

2 rainbow trout, cleaned

1 Tbsp unsalted butter

1 Tbsp chopped fresh dill

Sea salt

Preheat the oven to 450°F (230°C).

In a bowl, toss the tomatoes, onion, fennel, and lemon slices with enough olive oil to coat evenly, then season with kosher salt and pepper. Arrange in a single layer on a baking sheet. Roast just until the vegetables start to caramelize, about 20 minutes. Let cool to room temperature. Reduce the oven temperature to 350°F (180°C).

Cut out 2 squares of parchment paper, each about three times larger than each trout. Fold each square in half, then unfold it and lay it flat. Season the outsides of both trout with kosher salt and pepper. Using the fold mark as a guide, lay a trout on half of a square. Slip half of the roasted vegetables into the cavity, along with half each of the butter and dill. Fold the uncovered half of the parchment over the fish and, starting near the folded edge, fold the corner over, forming a triangle. Continue folding over the edge, making small overlapping folds, to seal the fish tightly in the packet. Repeat with the second parchment square, fish, and stuffing.

Place the parchment packets in a 9-by-13-inch (23-by-33-cm) baking dish. Roast until the fish is just cooked through, 15–20 minutes.

Carefully unwrap the parchment (there may be very hot steam inside) and serve the trout right away, with lemon wedges and sea salt on the side.

BOUILLABAISSE
with red pepper rouille

When researching bouillabaisse, we discovered you have to be a fourth-generation fisherman
who has been preparing bouillabaisse his whole life in order to make it authentically.
Now, we can't even pretend this is a "real" bouillabaisse. But what really is "real" anyway, right?
The recipe we created for you is an easy and mad tasty fish stew made by two dudes
living in New York who grew up approximately four thousand miles from Marseille.

red pepper rouille

¼ cup (½ oz/15 g) day-old small sourdough bread chunks without crusts

1 clove garlic, roughly chopped

2 Tbsp minced roasted red peppers

1 Tbsp rice vinegar

1 Tbsp cider vinegar

1 cup (8 fl oz/250 ml) vegetable oil

2 Tbsp ice water

2 Tbsp extra-virgin olive oil

2 leeks, white part only, thinly sliced

½ fennel bulb, trimmed, cored, and diced

2 plum tomatoes, diced

2 ribs celery, diced

1 garlic clove, minced

1 cup (8 fl oz/250 ml) dry white wine

1 lb (500 g) littleneck or similar clams, scrubbed

4 hake or pollock fillets, each about ¼ lb (125 g)

Kosher salt

¼ cup (⅓ oz/10 g) chopped mixed fresh herbs such as parsley, cilantro, tarragon, chervil, and mint

Coarse country bread slices, toasted, for serving

To make the rouille, combine the bread, garlic, red peppers, and vinegars in a food processor and process until smooth. With the motor running, slowly drizzle in the vegetable oil in a thin, steady stream and process until the mixture emulsifies. Then, as the mixture thickens, add the ice water and continue to process to achieve a texture similar to that of whipped butter. Taste and adjust the seasoning. Transfer to a bowl, cover, and refrigerate until ready to use.

In a small soup pot, heat the olive oil over low heat. Add the leeks, fennel, tomatoes, and celery and cook, stirring occasionally, until the vegetables soften, about 30 minutes.

Raise the heat to medium, add the garlic, wine, and 2 cups (8 fl oz/500 ml) water, and cook for 2 minutes. Add the clams, cover, and cook until the first clam opens, about 8 minutes. Add the fish, cover, and continue cooking, transferring the clams as they open to 4 bowls, until the fish is just cooked through, 5–7 minutes. Discard any clams that fail to open. Taste the broth and adjust with salt if necessary.

Transfer the fish to the bowls and ladle the broth on top. Garnish with the herbs. Spread the rouille on the toasted bread and serve alongside.

BEEF
bourguignon

When you go to the store to shop for this recipe, make sure you buy an extra bottle of wine. While you are preparing the recipe (which isn't the quickest one in the book), begin consuming the wine. Pick an appropriate soundtrack, such as Steely Dan or Joni Mitchell. Make sure you are about halfway through the bottle of wine when the beef begins to simmer. Turn the heat under the stew down to low and retire to the couch for a brief nap. When you wake up, like magic . . . the beef stew will be ready.

½ lb (250 g) slab bacon, cut into ½-inch (12-mm) lardons or very thick matchsticks

1 lb (500 g) beef chuck, cut into 1-inch (2.5-cm) pieces

Kosher salt and freshly ground pepper

1 lb (500 g) carrots, peeled and cut diagonally into 1-inch (2.5-cm) pieces

2 yellow onions, sliced

1 lb (500 g) button or mixed wild mushrooms, brushed clean, stemmed, and halved or quartered if large

2 garlic cloves, minced

1 Tbsp tomato paste

3 Tbsp all-purpose flour

3 Tbsp unsalted butter

1 bottle (750 ml) good-quality dry red wine

2 cups (16 fl oz/500 ml) beef stock

1 tsp fresh thyme leaves

Fresh lemon juice, as needed

4 slices sourdough bread, drizzled with olive oil, broiled, and rubbed with a garlic clove

In a Dutch oven or other large, heavy-bottomed pot, cook the bacon over medium heat, stirring occasionally, until lightly browned and some fat has rendered out, about 10 minutes. Using a slotted spoon, transfer the bacon to paper towels to drain.

Season the beef with salt and pepper. Working in batches to avoid crowding, add the beef to the hot bacon fat in the pot and sear, turning occasionally, until browned, about 5 minutes. Using a slotted spoon, transfer the beef to the plate with the bacon.

Raise the heat to high. Working in batches to avoid crowding, add the carrots, onions, and mushrooms to the pot and sauté until nicely browned, about 10 minutes. Add the garlic and tomato paste and sauté for 2 minutes. Using a slotted spoon, transfer the vegetables to a bowl.

Toss the beef and bacon with the flour, return them to the pot, and reduce the heat to medium. Cook, stirring, until the flour is browned, about 8 minutes. Add the butter and cook, stirring often, for 5 minutes longer. Add the wine and stock, cover, and cook over low heat until the beef is starting to become tender, 1–2 hours (check the meat after 1 hour of cooking and continue checking every 15–20 minutes).

Add the reserved vegetables and the thyme and cook until the beef and vegetables are tender, about 30 minutes longer. Add a splash of lemon juice, then taste and adjust the seasoning.

Serve the stew with the toasted bread.

DUCK
à l'orange

We decided this classic dish needed a massive overhaul. During our research, we unearthed classified documents indicating that another classic dish included orange and poultry as well, and that's the Chinese orange chicken available at pretty much every Chinese restaurant on the planet. So, in the spirit of the 1990s, turn up the NSYNC because here's some fusion cuisine. The end result is perfectly cooked and sliced duck breast with our version of a soy-orange glaze. Orange Chicken + Duck à l'Orange = A new classic! Zang!

marinade & sauce

2 oranges

¼ cup (2 oz/60 g) firmly packed light brown sugar

¼ cup (2 fl oz/60 ml) cider vinegar

¼ cup (2 fl oz/60 ml) soy sauce

2 garlic cloves, minced

2 Tbsp peeled and chopped fresh ginger

½ tsp freshly ground white pepper

2 large boneless duck breasts, about 2 lb (1 kg) total weight

1 shallot, minced

1 small jalapeño chile, cut into slices ¼ inch (6 mm) thick

2 green onions, white and tender green parts only, cut into 1-inch (2.5-cm) pieces

¼ cup (2 fl oz/60 ml) chicken stock

1 Tbsp cornstarch dissolved in ¼ cup (2 fl oz/60 ml) chicken stock

Steamed rice for serving

To make the marinade and sauce, using a vegetable peeler, remove the zest from the oranges and put in a bowl. Juice the oranges and add the juice to the bowl along with the brown sugar, vinegar, soy sauce, garlic, ginger, and white pepper. Transfer half of the mixture to a small bowl to use for the sauce; cover and refrigerate. Combine the remaining mixture with the duck breasts in a zippered plastic bag or airtight container. Refrigerate for at least 2 hours or preferably overnight.

Preheat the oven to 300°F (150°C).

Remove the duck breasts from the marinade and pat dry; discard the marinade. Using a paring knife, score the skin by making slices ¼ inch (6 mm) deep, spacing them about ½ inch (12 mm) apart. Be careful not to cut into the meat.

In an ovenproof sauté pan large enough to fit the duck breasts, place the breasts skin side down. Place the pan over low heat and cook the duck, allowing the fat to melt very slowly, for about 15 minutes, pouring off the fat as it accumulates in the pan. (You can reserve the fat for another use, such as cooking potatoes.) Transfer the pan to the oven and cook for 10 minutes, then check for doneness; an instant-read thermometer inserted into the thickest part of a breast should register 135°F (57°C). If it does not, continue cooking until done. Transfer the duck to a wire rack set over a baking sheet and let rest.

Pour off the excess fat from the pan and place the pan over medium-high heat. When the pan is hot, add the shallot, jalapeño, and green onions and cook, stirring occasionally, until browned and softened, about 3 minutes. Add the reserved orange mixture, the stock, and the cornstarch mixture and bring to a simmer, stirring until lightly thickened. Taste and adjust the seasoning. Remove from the heat, strain the sauce through a fine-mesh sieve, and cover to keep warm.

To serve, thinly slice the duck breasts against the grain and arrange on a platter. Pour the warm sauce over the top. Serve with steamed rice.

future
CLASSICS

brand-spankin'-new Sussman bros dishes

THAT ONE DAY WILL BE CLASSICS

CHICORY-PECAN SALAD
with maple vinaigrette

Great Scott! What's a chicory, you ask, Marty? Endive, escarole, and radicchio make up the tasty and overlooked chicory family. We love them because they have beautiful shapes and colors and are slightly bitter. We're sure that in 1955 everybody just drank milk shakes and ate steaks all day. But it's the twenty-first century. Time to start being healthy if you want to make the cut when they determine who gets to achieve eternal life on the Mars colony, Utopia.

1 cup (4 oz/125 g) pecans

½ cup (4 oz/125 g) sugar

1 Tbsp extra-virgin olive oil

½ tsp kosher salt

¼ tsp cayenne pepper

1 tart red apple such as Pink Lady

Juice of 1 lemon

¼ cup (2 fl oz/60 ml) walnut or extra-virgin olive oil

2 Tbsp cider vinegar

2 Tbsp maple syrup

1 head Belgian endive, leaves separated and cut into bite-size pieces

1 head radicchio, leaves separated and cut into bite-size pieces

1 head frisée, cut into bite-size pieces

1 bunch baby dandelion greens, cut into bite-size pieces

¼ cup (1 oz/30 g) shaved Piave or similar hard cheese

Preheat the oven to 350°F (180°C). Line a baking sheet with parchment paper or a nonstick baking mat.

In a bowl, toss the pecans with the sugar, olive oil, salt, and cayenne. Spread in a single layer on the prepared baking sheet. Toast in the oven until the pecans are fragrant and the sugar melts slightly, 10–15 minutes. Let cool to room temperature, then coarsely chop.

Halve and core the apple, then cut into thin slices. Transfer to a small bowl and toss with the lemon juice.

In another small bowl, whisk together the walnut oil, vinegar, and maple syrup to make a vinaigrette.

In a large bowl, toss the endive, radicchio, frisée, dandelion greens, pecans, and apples with the vinaigrette. Arrange on a platter, top with the cheese, and serve right away.

mostly
VEGETABLE DUMPLINGS
with spicy dipping sauce

At Bun-ker Vietnamese in Queens, a remarkable restaurant (that achieves the incredible feat of taking you back in time but also into the future of what a New York restaurant can be), the kitchen makes a *bánh xèo*—basically a crispy rice flour omelet—that's completely addictive. We crave it all day, every day. So we took elements of that amazing dish, a green onion pancake, and fried gyoza and created a perfect experiment of something we could call our own. The Sussman Brothers, appropriating cultures and wrapping them up in a nice little flavor packet since 2015.

dipping sauce

2 tsp fish sauce

1 Tbsp rice vinegar

1 tsp firmly packed light brown sugar

1 tsp Sriracha sauce

batter

1¼ cups (6½ oz/200 g) rice flour

2 Tbsp corn flour

1½ cups (12 fl oz/375 ml) coconut milk

1¼ cups (10 fl oz/310 ml) ice water

½ cup (1½ oz/45 g) thinly sliced green onions, white and tender green parts only

½ white onion, finely diced

1 small red bell pepper, seeded and diced

½ cup (1½ oz/45 g) shredded napa cabbage

1 cup (1 oz/30 g) *each* fresh mint and cilantro leaves

1 cup (3½ oz/105 g) bean sprouts

½ cup (2½ oz/75 g) shredded peeled carrots

2 Tbsp peeled and minced fresh ginger

1 Tbsp minced garlic

2 Tbsp fish sauce

1 Tbsp hoisin sauce

1 Tbsp soy sauce

Vegetable oil for frying

1 lime, quartered

To make the dipping sauce, in a small bowl, whisk together the fish sauce, rice vinegar, brown sugar, 1 tablespoon water, and the Sriracha. Set aside.

To make the batter, in a bowl, whisk together the rice flour, corn flour, coconut milk, ice water, and green onions until well combined. Cover with plastic wrap and refrigerate for 1 hour.

In a large bowl, stir together the white onion, bell pepper, cabbage, mint, cilantro, bean sprouts, carrots, ginger, garlic, fish sauce, hoisin sauce, and soy sauce. Set aside to use as the filling.

In a nonstick frying pan, heat about 1 tablespoon vegetable oil over medium-high heat and swirl to coat the bottom of the pan.

Using a spoon, drop dollops (each about 1 tablespoon) of the batter into the hot pan, spacing them evenly so they do not touch. Cook until they begin to turn golden brown and crispy around the edges and are opaque on top, about 3 minutes. Place 1 teaspoon of the filling on one-half of each batter round, then fold the other half over to enclose the filling like a tiny omelet. Cook for about 1 minute longer; the dumplings should be dry enough to hold together, like a crepe. Transfer the dumplings to a plate and repeat with the remaining batter and filling, using about 1 tablespoon oil to fry each batch.

Serve the dumplings right away, accompanied with the lime quarters and the dipping sauce.

BRUSSELS SPROUTS
with sunny-side eggs & dijon

Even after the fallout from atomic war, health fanatics will be wandering around in radiation suits still obsessing over which superfoods are the best. Brussels sprouts—a superfood—have found their spot in the "any preparation is tasty" pantheon: raw, shaved, roasted, and now, fried. These sprouts also have a fried egg on top, so while Brussels sprouts themselves are known as a superfood, the health fanatics will have to settle for this dish being just *super good food*.

1 Tbsp fresh lemon juice, plus more for apples

1 tsp honey

1 garlic clove, minced

2 tsp Dijon mustard

2 Tbsp balsamic vinegar

¼ cup (2 fl oz/60 ml) extra-virgin olive oil

4 cups (32 fl oz/1 l) vegetable oil

2 lb (1 kg) Brussels sprouts, trimmed and halved lengthwise

2 large eggs

Kosher salt and freshly ground pepper

1 cup (4 oz/125 g) walnuts, toasted and chopped

1 Granny Smith apple, cored, cut into small pieces, and tossed with fresh lemon juice

1 bunch green onions, white and tender green parts only, sliced on the diagonal

In a food processor, combine the lemon juice, honey, garlic, and mustard and blend until smooth. With the processor running, add the vinegar in a slow, steady stream. Then add the olive oil in a slow, steady stream while blending on medium high to form a smooth dressing.

In a large pot, heat the vegetable oil over medium-high heat to 350°F (180°C). When the oil begins to shimmer, working in batches if necessary to avoid crowding, add the Brussels sprouts and fry, stirring occasionally so they do not burn, until golden brown, about 3 minutes. Using a slotted spoon, transfer the Brussels sprouts to a paper towel–lined plate to drain.

Set a nonstick frying pan over medium heat. Carefully crack the eggs into the pan and cook until the whites are just set, 2–3 minutes for sunny-side up. Sprinkle with salt and pepper.

In a large serving bowl, toss the Brussels sprouts with the dressing, walnuts, apple, and half of the green onions. Top with the fried eggs and the remaining green onions. Just before serving, break the eggs up and mix into the salad, if desired. Don't be greedy; share the eggs. Alternatively, two hearty eaters who really like their Brussels sprouts can divide the salad in half and each enjoy a whole egg.

ROASTED CARROT & PISTACHIO SALAD
with fig balsamic vinaigrette

Back in 1955, or maybe even in 1985, salads were required to be green iceberg lettuce
with beefsteak tomatoes. Things have sure changed. Rock music, flying DeLoreans,
plutonium available at every corner drugstore . . . and salad made with just greens?
That's an idea that belongs in the past. We're going to the future. Greens?
Where we're going, salads don't need greens.

1 cup (8 fl oz/250 ml) extra-virgin olive oil,
plus 1 Tbsp

1 shallot, minced

¼ cup (2 fl oz/60 ml) balsamic vinegar

½ cup (2½ oz/75 g) diced fresh figs

Kosher salt

2 lb (1 kg) multicolored small carrots,
halved lengthwise

1 head radicchio

½ cup (2 oz/60 g) pistachios, roughly
chopped

Preheat the oven to 375°F (190°C).

In a large bowl, whisk together half of the olive oil, the shallot, vinegar, figs,
2 tablespoons water, and ½ teaspoon salt to make a vinaigrette.

In a large bowl, toss the carrots with the remaining olive oil and season with salt.
Spread in a single layer on a baking sheet and add ¼ cup (2 fl oz/60 ml) water. Roast
until the carrots begin to brown and crisp on the edges, about 20 minutes.

Meanwhile, roughly chop the radicchio, discarding the core. Peel the leaves apart.
Place half of the leaves in a large bowl. Set aside.

When the carrots are almost ready, in a frying pan, heat the 1 tablespoon olive oil
over high heat. Add the remaining radicchio and cook, stirring, until it wilts and
begins to brown in spots, about 2 minutes.

Transfer the cooked radicchio to the bowl holding the uncooked radicchio. Add
the carrots and mix gently using tongs. Add the pistachios, drizzle the vinaigrette
over the top, and toss to coat the vegetables evenly. Serve right away.

corn bread & brisket
PATTY MELT

Every once in a while we just have to pat ourselves on the back for doing something we haven't seen in other cookbooks. We aren't entirely sure we're the first to make a brisket patty melt using corn bread, but we are sure this is the best version out there. A vast improvement on the close-to-perfect patty melt is enough to make us feel pretty good about this one. When you start seeing this on the menu of every chain restaurant in America in five years, just remember who thought of it first.

brisket

2 lb (1 kg) beef brisket

1 Tbsp extra-virgin olive oil

Kosher salt

1 yellow onion, finely diced

1 garlic clove, minced

1 tsp firmly packed light brown sugar

1 Tbsp tomato paste

2 cups (16 fl oz/500 ml) chicken stock

Pinch of red pepper flakes

corn bread

Olive oil spray

1¼ cups (6¼ oz/195 g) cornmeal

1 cup (5 oz/155 g) all-purpose flour

1½ tsp baking powder

2 tsp kosher salt

2 Tbsp firmly packed light brown sugar

3 serrano chiles, seeded and minced

4 green onions, minced

1½ cups (12 fl oz/375 g) whole milk

½ cup (4 oz/125 g) whole-milk yogurt

½ cup (4 fl oz/125 ml) extra-virgin olive oil

1 large egg, beaten

1 Tbsp extra-virgin olive oil

1 small red onion, cut into thick rounds

4 slices Gruyère cheese

Unsalted butter for frying

To make the brisket, cut the meat into 1-inch (2.5-cm) pieces. In a wide pot, heat the olive oil over high heat. When the oil is very hot, add the brisket and a pinch of salt and cook, stirring, until browned, about 5 minutes. Reduce the heat to medium, add the onion, and sauté until softened and caramelized, about 7 minutes. Add the garlic, brown sugar, and tomato paste and sauté for 3–4 minutes. Add the stock and red pepper flakes and bring to a simmer. Reduce the heat to low, cover, and simmer until the meat is falling apart and tender, 2–3 hours. Add water if the pan begins to dry. The meat should be just barely covered with liquid when it is ready. If there is too much liquid at the end, transfer the liquid to a small saucepan and simmer until reduced.

To make the corn bread, preheat the oven to 375°F (190°C). Line a 9-inch (23-cm) square baking pan with parchment paper and spray with olive oil.

In a large bowl, stir together the cornmeal, flour, baking powder, salt, brown sugar, chiles, and green onions. In another bowl, whisk together the milk, yogurt, and olive oil. Add the milk mixture to the cornmeal mixture and fold just until the batter is blended; it will be slightly lumpy. Add the egg and fold until blended.

Pour the batter into the prepared pan. Bake until the bread is golden brown and a toothpick inserted into the center comes out clean, about 20 minutes. Transfer the pan to a wire rack and let cool completely.

Meanwhile, in a heavy frying pan, heat the olive oil over high heat. Add the onion and cook, turning once, until deeply caramelized, about 4 minutes on each side. Transfer to a cutting board and cut into ½-inch (12-mm) pieces.

Cut the corn bread into 4 equal pieces, then halve each piece horizontally. Place one-fourth of the braised beef on the cut side of a bottom piece of corn bread. Top with 1 tablespoon of the onion, a slice of cheese, and then the top piece of corn bread, cut side down. Repeat to make 3 more sandwiches. In a large nonstick frying pan, melt about 1 tablespoon butter over medium heat. Working in batches, fry the sandwiches, turning once and adding butter as needed, until the bread is browned and the cheese is melted, about 3 minutes on each side. Serve right away.

LAMB RIBS
with hot honey & lavender

We do consider ourselves inventors. Now, we haven't quite fallen off our toilet, hit our head, and come up with the flux capacitor here, but this recipe is still a pretty revolutionary invention. If our sweet-hot ratio calculations are correct, when each of these honey and lavender ribs hits your lips, you're gonna see some serious stuff. And if our theory of meat deliciousness is correct, your entire future hinges on your making these ribs.

2 large shallots, roughly chopped

4 garlic cloves

2-inch (5-cm) piece fresh ginger, peeled and roughly chopped

1 Tbsp extra-virgin olive oil

½ cup (6 oz/185 g) honey

2½ Tbsp kosher salt

1 Tbsp freshly ground white pepper

1–2 tsp cayenne pepper (depending how hot you like the ribs)

½ tsp dried lavender

2 racks lamb ribs, about 2 lb (1 kg) total weight

Fresh mint for garnish

Preheat the oven to 425°F (220°C).

In a bowl, toss together the shallots, garlic, ginger, and olive oil. Spread in a single layer on a baking sheet and roast until browned, 15–20 minutes. Reduce the oven temperature to 250°F (120°C).

Let the shallot mixture cool slightly. Transfer to a food processor, add the honey, salt, white pepper, cayenne, and lavender, and purée until smooth.

Rub the honey mixture evenly on the lamb racks. Place the racks, meaty side up, on a wire rack set on a rimmed baking sheet. Roast until tender, 3–4 hours. Remove from the oven, cut the ribs apart, and eat immediately. Or let the racks cool, scrape off the excess rub, and rewarm the racks under the broiler or over a hot grill until the outside is crispy and the inside is warm, then cut apart just before serving. Garnish with the mint and serve right away.

PORK BURGER
with apple ketchup

If you could time travel in a DeLorean back to, say, 1955, Des Plaines, Illinois, you could seize the opportunity to walk up to Ray Kroc and make an investment in a little burger chain that would eventually take over the world. But you can't do that because Doc Brown ain't real. But you can be part of burger history again. Follow the instructions that we've included here and you'll be one of the first to taste the reinvented burger of the future.

burgers

1 lb (500 g) ground pork

½ lb (250 g) ground beef (75% lean)

¼ cup (⅓ oz/10 g) panko bread crumbs

2 Tbsp Worcestershire sauce

1 large egg, beaten

2 garlic cloves, minced

1½ tsp kosher salt

1 tsp freshly ground pepper

1 tsp minced fresh thyme

¼ tsp dried sage

apple ketchup

4 Pink Lady or Honeycrisp apples

¼ cup (2 fl oz/60 ml) cider vinegar

1 tsp *each* ground cinnamon, ground ginger, and kosher salt

Pinch of ground cloves

quick slaw

2 cups (6 oz/185 g) shredded red cabbage

¼ cup (2 fl oz/60 ml) cider vinegar

Kosher salt

1 Tbsp extra-virgin olive oil

2 Tbsp vegetable oil

Kosher salt

2 Tbsp unsalted butter

4 hamburger buns, split

Mayonnaise for serving

To make the burgers, in a large bowl, combine the pork, beef, panko, Worcestershire, egg, garlic, salt, pepper, thyme, and sage. Mix gently with your hands just until combined; you don't want to overwork the meat. Shape into 4 patties, each about ¼ inch (6 mm) thick, and refrigerate until ready to cook.

To make the apple ketchup, peel, core, and chop the apples. In a saucepan, combine the apples, vinegar, cinnamon, ginger, salt, and cloves and bring to a simmer over low heat. Simmer, stirring occasionally, until the apples break down and the mixture thickens and is deep golden brown, 30–45 minutes. Remove from the heat and cover to keep warm.

To make the slaw, put the cabbage in a bowl. In a small bowl, whisk together the vinegar, 2 teaspoons salt, and the olive oil. Add to the cabbage and toss to coat. Taste and adjust the seasoning and set aside.

Preheat the oven to 400°F (200°C).

In a cast-iron frying pan, warm the vegetable oil over medium-high heat. Sprinkle the pork burgers on both sides with salt and place in the pan. Cook without disturbing for 2 minutes to allow a crust to develop. Flip the burgers and cook on the other side for 2 minutes. Then add the butter, allowing it to melt across the bottom of the pan. Transfer the pan to the oven and cook until an instant-read thermometer inserted into the center of a burger registers 160°F (70°C) for medium, about 3 minutes.

Remove the burgers from the oven and let rest while you toast the buns.

Spread a layer of mayonnaise on the bottom of each bun, then place a burger on top. Spread some apple ketchup on the burgers and top with the slaw (store any extra apple ketchup covered in the refrigerator for up to 1 month). Close the burgers with the bun tops and eat right away.

the ultimate
SMOOTHIE

The future is now. Barack and Hillary have blazed a trail, leaving the door wide open. And you might be asking us, Okay, future boys, who's the next president? How does Commander in Chief Justin Timberlake sound? By the time JT installs a recording studio in the West Wing, we'll all be consuming our meals via smoothies and fuel tablets, and only fringe society will take pleasure in food consumption. So if in twenty years JT becomes the sexiest, sleekest POTUS ever, shouldn't our daily smoothie follow suit and fill us up with some style?

peanut butter–almond

2 cups (16 fl oz/500 ml) almond milk

2 Tbsp peanut butter

½ tsp ground cinnamon

½ tsp ground nutmeg

½ tsp almond extract

½ banana, peeled and quartered

2 Tbsp chia seeds

1 Tbsp honey

1 tsp maca powder

1 tsp coconut oil

1 tsp hemp protein powder

lime–goji berry–kiwifruit

½ cup (1½ oz/45 g) chopped kale leaves

2 Tbsp goji berries

1 kiwifruit, peeled and coarsely chopped

Juice of 1 lime

1 cup (8 oz/250 g) crushed ice

1 Granny Smith apple, peeled, cored, and cut into chunks

½ cup (4 fl oz/125 ml) apple juice

1 oz (30 g) wheatgrass (optional)

1 tsp honey (optional)

1 avocado, pitted, peeled, and quartered

PEANUT BUTTER–ALMOND

In a blender, combine the almond milk, peanut butter, cinnamon, nutmeg, almond extract, banana, chia seeds, honey, maca powder, coconut oil, and protein powder and blend until smooth. Pour into 2 glasses.

LIME–GOJI BERRY–KIWIFRUIT

In a blender, combine the kale, goji berries, kiwi, lime juice, ice, apple, apple juice, wheatgrass (if using), honey (if using), and avocado and blend until smooth. Pour into 2 glasses.

STRATEGY FOR MAKING MONEY.

It takes old movies and remakes them louder and bigger, with more explosions and fancy CGI. They cost a lot more to film, market, and release. And we're doing the same thing for these dips. We started with the original and injected each with some Hollywood blockbuster juice. Bigger! Spicier! Fattier! More layers! More proteins! More calories! In surround sound! And, yes, these dips now include 3D glasses! If you haven't caught on yet, the whole point of this cookbook is to take classics and reimagine them in a new, modern, easy-to-execute way. At first we were met with some pushback, as lots of people believe certain food items are just "too classic" and "too iconic" to be revised. But there's no preciousness for us when it comes to food. Leave no food item unmessed with is what we say. (If *Batman* can be remade ninety-four times, we can redo some dips, right?)

SO IN THAT SPIRIT, HERE ARE YOUR

HOT SUMMER BLOCKBUSTER DIPS.

BACON-GUACAMOLE SALSA VERDE DIP

3 thin strips bacon, cut into ½-by-¼-inch (12-by-6-mm) pieces

4 jalapeño chiles

½ yellow onion, thinly sliced

1 garlic clove

2 tomatillos

1 ripe avocado, pitted, peeled, cut into small pieces, and tossed with fresh lemon juice

1 bunch fresh cilantro, leaves and stems chopped

Kosher salt

1 bag chicharrones (pork rinds) for serving

serves 4

(deep sexy voice-over) Sometimes love happens when you least expect it. In a city where life moves pretty fast, two flavors will find each other. This summer, fall in love with "When bacon meets guacamole." "I'll have what she's having!"

Preheat the broiler.

In a nonstick frying pan, cook the bacon over medium heat until the fat is rendered and the bacon is crisp, about 4 minutes. Using a slotted spoon, transfer to paper towels to drain.

Place the jalapeños, onion, garlic, and tomatillos on a rimmed baking sheet. Broil until browned, charred in spots, and slightly softened, 15–20 minutes. Let cool completely in the refrigerator.

Halve and seed the jalapeños. Combine the jalapeños, onion, garlic, tomatillos, avocado, cilantro, ¼ cup (2 fl oz/60 ml) water, and 2 teaspoons salt in a food processor and pulse until combined but still slightly chunky. Taste and adjust the seasoning.

Transfer the guacamole to a bowl and garnish with the bacon. Serve with the chicharrones for dipping.

SHRIMP CEVICHE 8-LAYER DIP

1 lb (500 g) shrimp, peeled, deveined, and cut into ¼-inch (6-mm) pieces

1 fresh jalapeño chile, seeded and sliced

½ cup (4 fl oz/125 ml) fresh lime juice

¼ cup (2 fl oz/60 ml) extra-virgin olive oil, plus 2 Tbsp

1 tsp kosher salt

1½ cups (9 oz/280 g) fresh corn kernels (from about 3 ears)

4 corn tortillas, halved

1 cup (8 fl oz/250 ml) store-bought salsa verde

1 avocado, pitted, peeled, and cut into chunks

1 cup (8 oz/250 g) sour cream or crème fraîche

1 cup (5 oz/155 g) pitted and sliced Castelvetrano olives

1 can (15 oz/425 g) black beans, rinsed and drained

1 cup (6 oz/188 g) pickled jalapeño chiles

1 cup (5 oz/155 g) crumbled queso fresco

Tortilla chips for serving

serves 4

(intense voice-over) In a world where six or even seven layers are not enough, a final layer will rise. From the ashes of failure, a new dip will emerge. One dip is destined to be a star. One dip will recognize its own greatness. One dip will save the galaxy. One dip will get the girl. One dip will break all the rules. This summer: Eight-Layer Dip.

Put the shrimp and fresh jalapeño in a shallow bowl. In a small saucepan, combine the lime juice, the ¼ cup (2 fl oz/60 ml) olive oil, and the salt and bring to a boil over high heat. Pour over the shrimp and jalapeño. Let cool in the refrigerator for about 30 minutes. Just before using, drain slightly.

In a large sauté pan, heat the 2 tablespoons olive oil over medium heat until smoking. Add the corn and sauté for 2 minutes. Using a slotted spoon, transfer to paper towels and let cool.

Heat a frying pan over medium heat. Working in batches to avoid crowding, add the tortillas and heat, turning once, until lightly toasted on both sides, about 1 minute on each side. Alternatively, one at a time, heat the tortillas over a gas flame on the stove top, turning as needed, until toasted on both sides.

In a food processor, combine the salsa verde and avocado and process until blended.

In a 9-inch (23-cm) square dish, evenly layer the ingredients in the following order: tortillas (with the cut side facing out to reach the edges of the dish), sour cream, olives, avocado salsa, beans, shrimp, corn, pickled jalapeños, and queso fresco.

Serve with the tortilla chips for dipping. When you get to the bottom, make tacos with the wet tortillas.

ULTRA MEGA DIP

½ cup (4 oz/125 g) sour cream

½ cup (4 fl oz/125 ml) mayonnaise

½ cup (4 fl oz/125 ml) buttermilk

2 Tbsp minced fresh dill

1 Tbsp minced fresh chives

2 Tbsp dried parsley

1 Tbsp *each* onion powder and garlic powder

1 tsp kosher salt

¼ tsp sweet Spanish paprika

¼ lb (125 g) blue cheese, crumbled

½ lb (250 g) shallots

2 cups (16 fl oz/500 ml) vegetable oil

Ridged potato chips for serving

serves 4

(impending doom voice-over) The greatest evil the world has ever faced has reached the shores of New York City. Three dips, all with personality quirks, readily digestible backstories that make them easy to love, and a long history of not getting along with one another, must put their personal problems aside and join forces to defeat evil. They are, the Ultra Mega Dip.

In a bowl, combine the sour cream, mayonnaise, buttermilk, dill, chives, parsley, onion powder, garlic powder, salt, and paprika and stir to mix well. Fold in the blue cheese.

Using a mandoline, slice the shallots into thin, even rounds about ⅛ inch (3 mm) thick.

In a saucepan, heat the vegetable oil over medium heat to 325°F (165°C). Add the shallots and fry until deep golden brown, about 10 minutes. Using a slotted spoon, transfer to paper towels to drain.

Sprinkle the shallots over the dip and serve with the potato chips for dipping.

worldwide CLASSICS

dishes from around the world that, due to a

EUROCENTRIC BIAS TO COOKING, AREN'T CONSIDERED CLASSICS BUT ARE

TARAMASALATA
with greek pita

We grew up eating lox spread on bagels but never knew about the awesome dip called *taramasalata*. It's a Greek dish usually made with carp roe, but we do it with trout roe here since that's easier to find and closer to our Jewish roots. Yes, roe is fish eggs, and don't fear: they are amazingly tasty. This unheralded classic is finally ready for its close-up.

¼ cup (½ oz/15 g) roughly torn sourdough bread without crust

Juice of 2 lemons

¼ tsp kosher salt

1 jar (3½ oz/105 g) trout roe

½ cup (4 fl oz/125 ml) extra-virgin olive oil

Small fresh dill sprigs for garnish

Pita chips for serving

In a food processor, combine the bread, lemon juice, and salt and pulse for 1 minute to mix well. Add 2 tablespoons of the trout roe and 1 tablespoon water. With the processor running, slowly drizzle in the olive oil, processing until emulsified. The mixture should resemble thin hummus or aioli and be a good consistency for spreading and dipping. If the mixture is too thick, add up to 1 tablespoon more water.

Transfer to a serving bowl and fold in 2 more tablespoons of the trout roe. Garnish with the remaining trout roe and a few dill sprigs. Serve the pita chips alongside.

KIBBEH
& tzatziki

These little pouches are like a one-two punch of awesome. A double whammy of delicious.
A secret song at the end of the album. A twenty-dollar bill in your front pocket you forgot about.
First, you get the crispy fried outside, then you hit the warm spicy inside. The flavors and textures
are so perfectly complementary. Don't be deterred if you've never served kibbeh before.
It's sure to become an instant classic in your house.

tzatziki

1 cup (8 oz/250 g) whole-milk Greek yogurt

1 Kirby cucumber, grated on the large holes
of a box grater

1 garlic clove, minced

½ tsp kosher salt

Juice of 1 lemon

Roughly chopped fresh dill for garnish

2 cups (12 oz/375 g) bulgur

1 Tbsp kosher salt

1 Tbsp ground cumin

2 tsp ground coriander

1 tsp sweet Spanish paprika

½ tsp cayenne pepper

1 Tbsp extra-virgin olive oil

2 lb (1 kg) ground beef or lamb

1 yellow onion, minced

¼ cup (1½ oz/45 g) golden raisins, minced

¼ cup (1¼ oz/40 g) pine nuts, toasted

1 small jalapeño chile, seeded and minced

2 garlic cloves, minced

Vegetable oil for deep-frying

To make the tzatziki, in a small bowl, stir together the yogurt, cucumber, garlic, salt, and lemon juice. Cover and refrigerate until ready to serve.

Put the bulgur in a bowl, add water to cover, and let soak for 30 minutes.

In a small bowl, stir together the salt, cumin, coriander, paprika, and cayenne.

In a wide sauté pan, heat the olive oil over medium heat. When the oil is hot, add half each of the beef, spice mixture, and onion and cook, stirring, until the beef is cooked through, about 5 minutes. Transfer to a bowl, add the raisins and pine nuts, and stir to combine. Cover and refrigerate the filling until ready to use.

Drain the bulgur and transfer to a food processor. Add the remaining beef, spice mixture, and onion along with the jalapeño and garlic. Pulse until a pastelike consistency forms. Transfer the bulgur mixture to a bowl.

Line a baking sheet with parchment paper.

To form the kibbeh, put 2 tablespoons of the bulgur mixture in the palm of your hand. Use your thumb to make a well in the center. Place a few teaspoons of the cooked beef filling in the well. Using your fingers, shape the bulgur mixture around the filling to enclose it, forming an oval. Place on the prepared baking sheet. Form the remaining kibbeh, placing them on the baking sheet as you go, then refrigerate the kibbeh.

Pour the oil into a pot to a depth of 3 inches (7.5 cm) and heat to 350°F (180°C). Add 3 or 4 kibbeh to the hot oil (leave enough space so they are not touching one other), and fry until browned and cooked through, 3–4 minutes. To test, remove an oval from the oil and break it open to see if it is fully cooked. If it is not, reduce the heat slightly and continue cooking until fully cooked. Using a slotted spoon, transfer to paper towels to drain. Repeat to fry the remaining kibbeh.

Sprinkle the tzatziki with the dill. Serve the kibbeh hot with the tzatziki alongside.

cold THAI NOODLES

You need to buy a bottle of fish sauce to make these Thai noodles. Do so now.
Keep it on hand at all times. Put a few drops on pretty much everything.
It's like a secret elixir or a magic potion of flavor powers. It will change your life.
Now that we've converted you to worshipping the fish sauce, on to the recipe.

dressing

1 Tbsp minced lemongrass, white part only

2 plum tomatoes, diced

1 red Fresno or jalapeño chile, seeded and diced

2 Tbsp fish sauce

3 Tbsp rice vinegar

1 Tbsp firmly packed light brown sugar

2 Tbsp extra-virgin olive oil

½ lb (250 g) rice noodles

1 cup (1½ oz/45 g) chopped fresh basil (preferably Thai basil)

1 cup (1½ oz/45 g) fresh cilantro leaves and minced stems

½-lb (250-g) block firm tofu, crumbled into ½-inch (12-mm) pieces

½ lb (250 g) bean sprouts

½ cup (3 oz/90 g) chopped toasted peanuts

To make the dressing, in a bowl, mix together the lemongrass, tomatoes, chile, fish sauce, vinegar, brown sugar, and olive oil.

Soak the rice noodles in hot water for 15 minutes or according to the package directions. Drain well.

In a bowl, combine the rice noodles, dressing, basil, cilantro, tofu, bean sprouts, and peanuts and toss to mix well. Let sit for 15 minutes to allow the flavors to come together. Toss again and serve.

ras el hanout RABBIT

We were inspired to include this recipe after eating the food at the Brooklyn restaurant of our friend Sara Kramer, a chef who garnered substantial acclaim for her rabbit dish. Even in intense food circles, rabbit is still an unappreciated protein. So it's no surprise that in the home-cooking world, rabbit hasn't quite come into vogue. So be the Anna Wintour of your kitchen, get ahead of the curve, and try some rabbit.

ras el hanout spice blend

1 Tbsp ground cumin

2 tsp ground cardamom

1½ tsp ground allspice

1 tsp ground ginger

1 tsp ground cinnamon

1 tsp cayenne pepper

1 tsp ground nutmeg

1 tsp ground turmeric

1 tsp kosher salt

1 tsp freshly ground black pepper

1 tsp freshly ground white pepper

½ tsp ground mace

½ tsp ground cloves

½ tsp ground anise

5 Tbsp (3 fl oz/80 ml) extra-virgin olive oil, plus ½ cup (4 fl oz/125 ml)

8 rabbit legs

8 cups (64 fl oz/2 l) chicken stock

1 cup (6 oz/185 g) bulgur

2 cups (16 fl oz/500 ml) boiling water

1 pint (12 oz/375 g) cherry tomatoes, halved

½ cup (3 oz/90 g) golden raisins

½ cup (2½ oz/75 g) pine nuts, toasted

½ cup (½ oz/15 g) *each* fresh flat-leaf parsley and mint leaves, roughly chopped

¼ cup (2 fl oz/60 ml) fresh lemon juice

To make the spice blend, in a small bowl, stir together the cumin, cardamom, allspice, ginger, cinnamon, cayenne, nutmeg, turmeric, salt, black pepper, white pepper, mace, cloves, and anise.

In a Dutch oven, heat 4 tablespoons (2 fl oz/60 ml) of the olive oil over over medium-high heat. Sprinkle the rabbit legs on the skin side with one-fourth of the spice blend. Place the legs, skin side down, in the pan and cook until golden brown, about 5 minutes. Add the stock and stir in half of the remaining spice blend (reserve the remainder for another use). Bring to a simmer, cover, and cook over low heat for 45 minutes.

Meanwhile, put the bulgur in a bowl and pour the boiling water over it. Cover with plastic wrap and let sit for 10 minutes.

In a frying pan, heat 1 tablespoon of the olive oil over medium-high heat. Add the cherry tomatoes and cook until they begin to blister and sear, about 2 minutes. Remove from the heat.

Drain the bulgur and place in a bowl. Add the cherry tomatoes, raisins, pine nuts, parsley, mint, lemon juice, and the ½ cup (4 fl oz/125 ml) olive oil and stir to mix well.

After 40 minutes, check the rabbit for doneness; an instant-read thermometer inserted into the thickest part, away from the bone, should register 160°F (71°C).

Using a slotted spoon or tongs, transfer the rabbit to a platter. Place the pot with the sauce over high heat, bring to a boil, and cook until the sauce is reduced by half and has become a thick, sticky glaze, about 7 minutes.

Spoon the bulgur onto the platter with the rabbit, then pour the sauce over the bulgur and rabbit. Serve right away.

CHICKPEA MASALA
& saffron rice

The flavors of curry, chickpeas, and rice are so insanely well paired that we had
no choice but to include this recipe. Not to mention that this is one of the
quickest recipes in the book to put together. So, if you're short on time
but need a full meal, this is the time to stop flipping the pages.

1 Tbsp ground cumin

1/4 tsp saffron threads

1 cup (7 oz/220 g) basmati rice

1 3/4 cups (14 fl oz/430 ml) chicken or
vegetable stock or water

Kosher salt

1 Tbsp extra-virgin olive oil

1 small red onion, finely diced

1 garlic clove, minced

1 Tbsp peeled and minced fresh ginger

2 Tbsp curry powder

1/4 cup (2 fl oz/60 ml) heavy cream

1 can (15 1/2 oz/485 g) chickpeas,
rinsed and drained

3 oz (90 g) spinach

Juice of 1 lemon

1/2 cup (4 oz/125 g) whole-milk yogurt
seasoned with pepper and lightly drizzled
with extra-virgin olive oil (optional)

In a saucepan, combine the cumin and saffron over medium heat. Toast, stirring, until
fragrant and slightly darkened in color, about 2 minutes. Add the rice and stock and
season with 1/2 teaspoon salt, if desired. Raise the heat to high, cover, and bring to a
simmer. Reduce the heat to low and cook for 15 minutes. Remove from the heat and let
stand, covered, for 10 minutes. The rice will have absorbed the liquid and be tender.

Meanwhile, in a sauté pan, heat the olive oil over medium heat. Add the onion, garlic,
and ginger and cook, stirring, until softened, about 10 minutes. Add the curry powder
and cook, stirring, until aromatic, 3–4 minutes. Add the cream, 1/4 cup (2 fl oz/60 ml)
water, the chickpeas, and 1/2 teaspoon salt and stir to combine. Taste and adjust the
seasoning. Add the spinach and sauté until wilted, 2–3 minutes.

Spoon the rice onto plates and top with the curried chickpeas and spinach. Garnish
with the lemon juice and with the yogurt, if desired, and serve right away.

MAPO TOFU
with crispy chinese sausage

Mapo tofu is Max's Desert Island Meal. As in, if you have to live on a desert island and can have only one dish for the rest of your life, what would it be? That question doesn't make any sense. How could you be stuck on a desert island with a lifetime supply of mapo tofu, or any other dish, for that matter? Totally illogical question, same honest answer: mapo tofu.

1 cup (8 fl oz/250 ml) soy sauce

1 Tbsp fish sauce

2 Tbsp fermented black beans

2 Tbsp fermented chile bean paste

2 dried Thai chiles, or 1 tsp red pepper flakes

2 Tbsp freshly ground Sichuan peppercorns

2 Tbsp cornstarch dissolved in ¼ cup (2 fl oz/60 ml) water

1 Tbsp vegetable oil

1 lb (500 g) Chinese pork sausage (*lap cheong*), cut into slices ½ inch (12 mm) thick

2 packages (about 14 oz/440 g each) firm tofu, drained and cut into 1-inch (2.5-cm) cubes, at room temperature

2 bunches green onions, white and tender green parts only, thinly sliced on the diagonal

In a pot, combine 2 cups (16 fl oz/500 ml) water, the soy sauce, and fish sauce and bring to a boil over high heat. Add the black beans, chile paste, Thai chiles, and Sichuan pepper and return to a boil. Stir in the cornstarch mixture to thicken the sauce. Remove from the heat.

In a frying pan, heat the vegetable oil over medium heat. Add the sausage and cook, stirring with a wooden spoon every 30 seconds to prevent burning, until crispy, 3–5 minutes.

Add the sauce to the pan and cook for 1 minute. Add the tofu and gently stir, being careful to not break up the cubes, until coated with the sauce. Reduce the heat to low, cover, and cook for 5 minutes.

Serve in individual bowls topped with the green onions.

CHICKEN
on a stick

If there is one thing uniting all humans across different continents, languages, and cultures, it is chicken on a stick. Everywhere you go, people are grilling chicken on a stick. We hope that at some point, we will all stop our arguments and look up at the stars and realize, hey, we all share the same DNA and common ancestry. Let's stop all the fighting and work toward some common goals of the human race. We're really just one big family that loves chicken on a stick.

chicken

1 cup (8 oz/250 g) whole-milk yogurt

¼ cup (⅓ oz/10 g) chopped fresh cilantro stems and leaves

1 Tbsp fish sauce

1 Tbsp ground coriander

1 tsp ground cumin

1 tsp sweet Spanish paprika

½ tsp smoked paprika

½ tsp ground fennel

½ tsp ground turmeric

½ tsp ground cinnamon

1 red jalapeño chile, seeded and minced

1½ lb (750 g) boneless, skinless chicken breasts, cut into 1-inch (2.5-cm) pieces

hot sauce

6 green jalapeño chiles

½ white onion, sliced ½ inch (12 mm) thick

1 garlic clove, unpeeled

½ cup (¾ oz/20 g) chopped fresh cilantro stems and leaves

2 Tbsp sour cream

1 Tbsp extra-virgin olive oil

1 tsp kosher salt

To make the chicken, in a bowl, stir together the yogurt, cilantro, fish sauce, coriander, cumin, sweet paprika, smoked paprika, fennel, turmeric, cinnamon, red jalapeño, and 2 tablespoons water. Add the chicken and toss to coat with the marinade. Cover and refrigerate for at least 2 hours or preferably overnight.

To make the hot sauce, preheat the oven to 450°F (230°C).

Place the green jalapeños, onion, and garlic on a baking sheet. Roast until charred and softened, 15–20 minutes. Let cool, then remove the stems and seeds from the jalapeños and peel the garlic clove. In a food processor, combine the jalapeños, onion, garlic, cilantro, sour cream, olive oil, salt, and ¼ cup (2 fl oz/60 ml) water and blend until smooth, adding up to ¼ cup (2 fl oz/60 ml) more water as needed for desired spiciness and consistency. Taste and adjust the seasoning. (The hot sauce can be made up to 2 days in advance and refrigerated until ready to serve.)

Soak six 8-inch (20-cm) wooden skewers in water to cover for 30 minutes, then drain.

Build a hot fire in a charcoal grill or preheat a gas grill to high. Using a grill brush, scrape the heated grill rack clean and rub the rack with oil. Alternatively, preheat the broiler.

Remove the chicken from the marinade and thread the pieces onto the skewers, dividing evenly. Grill or broil the chicken, turning often to prevent charring or burning, until just cooked through, 10–12 minutes. Serve right away with the hot sauce.

puerto rican
MOFONGO

The conceptualization of this dish began with *mofongo*, a Puerto Rican classic that calls for mixing green plantains, *chicharrones*, and sometimes chicken or other ingredients, and seasonings. But from there we've gone in a much more modern direction. Instead of mashing everything together and forming the result into a ball, this is a plated dish with a citrus dressing that allows you to put all of the flavors together in each bite. We aren't sure how well this would go over during the Puerto Rican parade in Brooklyn, but for a new take on authentic flavors, we think we've nailed it.

4 boneless, skin-on chicken thighs, about 1½ lb (750 g) total weight

Kosher salt and freshly ground black pepper

2 Tbsp vegetable oil, plus 1 cup (8 fl oz/250 ml)

2 green plantains, peeled and cut into 2-inch (5-cm) chunks

1 garlic clove, mashed to a paste

¼ cup (2 fl oz/60 ml) extra-virgin olive oil

2 Tbsp fresh lemon juice

2 Tbsp fresh lime juice

1 tsp cayenne pepper

1 tsp ground coriander

½ cup (½ oz/15 g) fresh cilantro leaves, roughly chopped

½ cup (1 oz/28 g) packaged chicharrones (pork rinds)

Season the chicken with salt and black pepper. In a large frying pan, heat the 2 tablespoons vegetable oil over medium heat. Add the chicken and cook, turning once, until golden brown and cooked through, 10–15 minutes. Transfer to a plate and cover loosely with aluminum foil.

In a large saucepan, heat the 1 cup (8 fl oz/250 ml) vegetable oil to 350°F (180°C). Working in batches if necessary to avoid crowding, add the plantains and fry until crispy and golden brown, about 10 minutes. Using a slotted spoon, transfer to paper towels to drain briefly.

In a small bowl, whisk together the garlic, olive oil, lemon juice, lime juice, cayenne, coriander, and 2 teaspoons salt to make a dressing.

To serve, cut the chicken thighs against the grain into thick slices and place on a platter along with the plantains. Drizzle the dressing over the top. Sprinkle with the cilantro and chicharrones and serve right away.

STRIPED BASS
with red curry

When it comes to Thai food, Max is like one of those guys on the street who politely holds
the Bible and will try to convert you in the most gentle, sincere way. He won't mess
with your day or anything, but if asked, Max will sing the virtues of Thai food to anyone who will listen.
The rich flavors and aromatic elements of the broths and marinades are so dynamic, they truly
stand apart from all other cuisines. We hope that this recipe acts as an intro to cooking Thai food at home
(because there is more to the cuisine than what's on the menu at your neighborhood Thai place).

3 Tbsp extra-virgin olive oil,
plus more as needed

1 small red onion, minced

1 Tbsp peeled and minced fresh ginger

1 garlic clove, minced

2 Tbsp red curry paste

1½ cups (12 fl oz/375 ml) coconut milk

Juice of 2 limes

4-inch (10-cm) lemongrass stalk,
white part only

2 skin-on striped bass fillets,
each about 6 oz (185 g)

Kosher salt

1 cup (1 oz/30 g) fresh cilantro leaves

1 cup (5 oz/155 g) cooked wild rice,
kept warm

Preheat the oven to 375°F (190°C).

In a saucepan, heat 1 tablespoon of the olive oil over low heat. Add the onion, ginger, and garlic and cook, stirring often, until softened, about 10 minutes, adding a few more drops of olive oil if the ingredients start to stick.

Add the curry paste and sauté for 3–4 minutes. Add the coconut milk, lime juice, and lemongrass and bring to simmer. Remove from the heat and cover to keep warm. Discard the lemongrass before serving.

Pat the fish dry with paper towels and season lightly with salt. In a large, heavy frying pan, heat the remaining 2 tablespoons olive oil over medium-high heat. Add the fish, skin side down, and press lightly with the back of a large spoon to bring the skin in contact with the oil. Cook for 2 minutes, then transfer the pan to the oven and cook until the fish is opaque throughout, 4–7 minutes, depending on the thickness of the fish.

Spoon the curry sauce onto individual plates, top with the fish, and garnish with the cilantro. Serve the wild rice on the side.

breakfast
CLASSICS

the indisputable favorites

AT THEIR BEST

hash brown OMELET

What you are experiencing and tasting here is innovation. Who says an omelet must be made of eggs? Like the Snuggie or the Swiffer, this is a situation where a small tweak can change the way you see things forever. We're not saying this is akin to the caveman inventing the wheel, but making an omelet out of hash browns is nearly as revolutionary.

4 strips bacon

2 Tbsp maple syrup

2 large russet potatoes

3 Tbsp vegetable oil, plus more if needed

2 large eggs

Kosher salt and freshly ground pepper

Hot sauce or ketchup for serving

In a nonstick frying pan, cook the bacon over medium heat until crispy, 3–4 minutes on each side. After 5 minutes, pour the maple syrup over the bacon. When the bacon becomes sticky, transfer to a plate. Reserve the pan.

Using the medium holes on a box grater, grate the potatoes into a bowl. Squeeze to remove excess liquid. Do not rinse.

In a nonstick frying pan, heat the vegetable oil over medium heat. Press the grated potatoes tightly into the pan to form a circle; you don't want any gaps. Cook without disturbing for 3 minutes. Gently swirl the pan. If the entire disk of hash browns moves together without any sticking, you're in great shape.

Invert a plate over the pan, carefully invert the pan and plate together, lift off the pan, and then slide the omelet back into the pan. Cook the other side until deep golden brown, 2–3 minutes. Remove from the heat and keep warm.

Wipe out the pan used to cook the bacon and set it over medium heat. Carefully crack the eggs into the pan and cook until the whites are just set, about 3 minutes for sunny-side up. Sprinkle with salt and a grind of pepper.

Put the bacon and eggs on one-half of the hash brown omelet and gently fold the other half over to close. Using a spatula, slide the omelet out of the pan onto a plate. Serve right away with hot sauce.

FULL ENGLISH
breakfast sandwich

Every time we write a cookbook, we draw inspiration from chef April Bloomfield. She's one of the most talented chefs in the world, and our personal and professional connections to The Breslin restaurant have inspired and shaped our lives in very powerful ways. So as an homage to one of the living greats (hopefully she doesn't find this sandwich to be a travesty!), we present the Full English Breakfast Sandwich.

4 Tbsp (2 oz/60 g) unsalted butter

4 slices challah bread

4 strips bacon

2 sausage patties

1 beefsteak tomato, cut into 6 thick slices

1 can (15 oz/425 g) English-style baked beans in tomato sauce

Kosher salt

1 Tbsp white vinegar

2 large eggs

In a nonstick frying pan, melt the butter over medium heat. Add the challah and cook, turning once, until golden brown, about 1 minute on each side. Transfer to a plate.

Wipe out the pan with paper towels, then add the bacon and cook over medium heat until extra crispy, 3–4 minutes on each side. Transfer to paper towels to drain.

In the same pan, cook the sausage in the remaining bacon fat over medium heat, turning once, until golden brown and crispy, about 3 minutes on each side. Transfer to paper towels to drain.

In the same pan, cook the tomato slices over high heat, turning once, until they begin to brown, about 1 minute on each side. Transfer to a plate.

In a small saucepan over medium heat, warm the baked beans until bubbling, 8–10 minutes.

Fill a deep sauté pan two-thirds full of water, add 1 tablespoon salt and the vinegar, and bring to a gentle boil over high heat. Reduce the heat to a gentle simmer. Crack 1 egg into a ramekin and gently slide it into the simmering water. Repeat with the second egg. Cook until no runny white is visible but the yolks are still soft, 3–5 minutes. Using a slotted spoon, transfer the eggs to a plate.

To assemble each sandwich, stack 2 strips bacon, 3 tomato slices, 1 sausage patty, and 1 egg on a bread slice. Cover with half of the beans and a second bread slice. Serve right away with a fork and knife and many napkins.

gran' a' slama
BREAKFAST

As Andy Dufresne said in *The Shawshank Redemption*, "Get busy living, or get busy dying."
This waffle-sausage-egg breakfast sandwich perfectly encapsulates that saying because when you're
eating it, you're definitely livin'. But look at it and you'll know you're surely not doing your heart any favors.
So here's a "last meal" that's as filling as "3 hots." And all you'll need when you're done eating it is the cot.

waffle batter

3 cups (15 oz/470 g) all-purpose flour

¼ cup (2 oz/60 g) sugar

1 Tbsp ground cinnamon

4 tsp baking powder

¼ tsp kosher salt

2 large eggs

2 cups (16 fl oz/500 ml) whole milk

½ cup (4 fl oz/125 ml) vegetable oil

1 tsp *each* pure vanilla extract and almond extract

sausage

1½ lb (750 g) ground pork

Leaves from 2 fresh thyme sprigs

Leaves from 2 fresh rosemary sprigs

1 garlic clove, minced

1 tsp *each* dried sage and onion powder

2 large eggs, beaten

½ cup (¾ oz/20 g) panko bread crumbs

1 Tbsp Worcestershire sauce

peach compote

3 peaches, pitted and cut into 1-inch (2.5-cm) pieces

1 cup (8 oz/250 g) sugar

1 Tbsp vegetable oil, plus more for waffle iron

8 strips bacon

8 large eggs

To make the waffle batter, in a large bowl, whisk together the flour, sugar, cinnamon, baking powder, and salt. In a bowl, whisk the eggs until blended, then whisk in the milk, vegetable oil, and vanilla and almond extracts. Pour the milk mixture into the flour mixture and whisk until blended. Cover and refrigerate for at least 1 hour but preferably overnight.

To make the sausage, in a large bowl, combine the pork, thyme, rosemary, garlic, sage, onion powder, eggs, panko, and Worcestershire. Mix gently with your hands just until combined; you don't want to overwork the meat. Shape into 4 patties, place on a plate, cover, and refrigerate until ready to cook.

To make the peach compote, in a saucepan, combine ½ cup (4 fl oz/125 ml) water, the peaches, and the sugar and bring to a simmer over medium heat. Reduce the heat to low and cook until the peaches break down and the liquid evaporates, about 30 minutes. The mixture should be soft and jamlike. Remove from the heat.

Preheat the oven to 350°F (180°C). Preheat your waffle iron, then brush the top and bottom plates with oil. Following the manufacturer's directions, ladle some batter (usually ½–1 cup/125–250 ml, depending on the size of the waffle iron) onto the bottom plate just to cover, then close the lid. Cook the waffle until crisp and golden; the timing will depend on your iron. Transfer the waffle to a baking sheet and keep warm in the oven. Repeat with the remaining batter. You should have 8 waffles.

In a nonstick frying pan, cook the bacon over medium heat until crispy, 3–4 minutes per side. Transfer to paper towels to drain.

In another nonstick frying pan, heat the 1 tablespoon vegetable oil over medium-high heat. Add the sausage patties and cook, turning once, until crispy and browned, about 3 minutes on each side. Transfer to a plate and cover with aluminum foil.

Wipe out the bacon pan with paper towels. Set the pan over medium heat. Carefully crack 4 of the eggs into the pan and cook until the whites are just set, about 3 minutes for sunny-side up, then transfer to a plate. Repeat with the remaining 4 eggs.

Remove the waffles from the oven. To assemble each sandwich, place 1 waffle on a plate. Top with 1 sausage patty, 2 strips of bacon, 2 fried eggs, and a large dollop of the peach compote. Then top with another waffle. Serve right away.

east coast OMELET

It was a simple embrace of our Jewish roots and our geographical location that led to the creation of this East Coast omelet. Unlike its meat-focused Western brother, this version has all the appetizing elements of a Jewish brunch stuffed inside perfectly cooked eggs. And since there's no ham or meat, you quasi-kosher kids out there can go one meal without feeling the crushing guilt of your bubby's disappointment in your life choices.

3 Tbsp unsalted butter, at room temperature

4 large eggs

1 tsp whole milk

¼ lb (125 g) smoked whitefish fillet

2 oz (60 g) cream cheese, at room temperature

1 Tbsp chopped fresh chives

1 Tbsp finely chopped green onions, white and tender green parts only

½ cup (3 oz/90 g) cherry tomatoes, halved

1 red onion, sliced

1 Tbsp capers

Rye toast or bagels for serving

In a bowl, whisk together 2 tablespoons of the butter, the eggs, and the milk until well blended.

In another bowl, stir together the whitefish, cream cheese, chives, green onions, tomatoes, red onion, and capers.

In a nonstick frying pan, melt the remaining 1 tablespoon butter over low heat. Pour in the egg mixture and cook without disturbing for 3 minutes. As the eggs begin to change color slightly along the edges, use a spatula to pull the edges gently away from the pan sides. Then angle the pan away from you slightly and use the spatula to pull one edge of the cooked eggs away from the pan sides, allowing some of the uncooked eggs to flow underneath. Continue in this manner until all of the uncooked eggs have flowed underneath the set egg. This will take about 5 minutes longer. When the eggs are almost set to your desired consistency, use a spoon to smear the whitefish mixture onto one-half of the omelet.

Slide the omelet onto a plate, lifting the edge of the pan to flip the uncovered half over the whitefish mixture. Serve right away with rye toast.

SALAMI
& eggs

When we were young, our dad used to make us salami and eggs on the weekends. Soon we grew older and began making salami and eggs for ourselves on the weekends. And one day we'll be old and we will make salami and eggs for our kids on the weekends. *This* is what a recipe is for. *This* is what food is all about.

1 tsp vegetable oil, plus ¼ cup (2 fl oz/60 ml)

6 oz (185 g) deli or kosher-style dry salami, diced

2 shallots, thinly sliced

6 large eggs

½ tsp kosher salt

½ tsp freshly ground pepper

1 Tbsp unsalted butter

1 jalapeño chile, halved lengthwise, seeded, and cut into half-moons

1 bunch green onions, white and tender green parts only, chopped

Ketchup for serving

In a nonstick frying pan, heat the 1 teaspoon vegetable oil over medium heat. Add the salami and cook, stirring occasionally to avoid burning, until crisp, 3–4 minutes. Transfer to a small bowl.

In the same pan, heat the remaining ¼ cup (2 fl oz/60 ml) vegetable oil over medium heat. Add the shallots and cook, stirring occasionally to avoid burning, until golden brown, 5–7 minutes. Using a slotted spoon, transfer to paper towels to drain. Wipe out the pan with paper towels.

In a bowl, whisk together the eggs, salt, and pepper until well blended. Return the pan to medium heat and melt the butter. Pour in the eggs and cook without disturbing for 30 seconds. Then begin to slowly and gently move the eggs around with a spatula. Push from one side of the pan to the other in single long strokes, then redistribute the eggs back across the entire pan. "Slow and low" is the key to great scrambled eggs, so let them cook gently without too much fussing and moving them around. You are trying to avoid crispy edges or brown spots.

Once the eggs are almost cooked to your desired firmness, add the reserved salami and shallots and the jalapeño and mix in gently. The eggs should be light yellow and fluffy, with spots of fluffy white.

Spoon the eggs onto plates and serve right away, with the green onions and ketchup on the side.

BUTTERSCOTCH PANCAKES
with chocolate chunks

You've got a lame box of pancake mix sitting in the cupboard. And you could use that
and be left totally unsatisfied and underwhelmed. Or you could make these pancakes.
There is butterscotch *in and on* these pancakes. In. *And* on.
Take a moment . . . we knew you'd come around once you got all the facts.

butterscotch sauce

4 Tbsp (2 oz/60 g) unsalted butter

1/2 cup (3 1/2 oz/105 g) firmly packed dark brown sugar

1 cup (8 fl oz/250 ml) heavy cream

1/2 tsp kosher salt

1 tsp pure vanilla extract

pancakes

1 1/2 cups (7 1/2 oz/235 g) all-purpose flour

1 tsp baking powder

1 tsp kosher salt

2 large eggs, separated

1 cup (8 fl oz/250 ml) whole milk

1 cup (8 fl oz/250 ml) butterscotch sauce (recipe above)

Up to 4 Tbsp (2 oz/60 g) unsalted butter

1/2 cup (3 oz/90 g) bittersweet chocolate chips or chopped bittersweet chocolate

To make the butterscotch sauce, in a heavy-bottomed saucepan, melt the butter over medium heat. Add the brown sugar, cream, and salt and whisk until well blended. Bring to a very gentle simmer and cook, whisking occasionally, until the sugar is completely dissolved and is bubbling, about 5 minutes. Remove from the heat and let cool. Add the vanilla and stir to combine.

To make the pancakes, in a large bowl, whisk together the flour, baking powder, and salt.

In a bowl, using a whisk or an electric mixer, whip the egg whites until soft peaks form.

In another bowl, whisk together the milk, egg yolks, and butterscotch sauce. Pour the milk mixture over the flour mixture and fold to combine partially. Fold in the egg whites just until no visible flour remains; the mixture will still be lumpy.

In a large nonstick frying pan, melt 1 tablespoon butter over medium heat. Pour in 1/3 cup (3 fl oz/80 ml) batter for each pancake and sprinkle 1–2 teaspoons chocolate chips on top. Cook until bubbles form on the top, 2–3 minutes. Flip the pancakes and cook until golden on the bottom, about 2 minutes longer. Transfer the pancakes to a platter and keep warm in the oven. Repeat to cook the remaining pancakes, adding more butter as needed.

Serve the pancakes with the remaining butterscotch sauce.

cinnamon-sunflower seed
GRANOLA

When Eli made this granola for brunch at Mile End Delicatessen in Brooklyn,
several people asked him for the recipe, saying it was the best granola they'd ever had.
Humbled by that possibly truthful statement, we're sharing the recipe here
because no one should keep such a good thing like this a secret.

8 cups (1½ lb/750 g) rolled oats

½ cup (2 oz/60 g) walnuts, toasted and roughly chopped

½ cup (2 oz/60 g) almonds, toasted and roughly chopped

¼ cup (1 oz/30 g) sunflower seeds

¼ cup (1 oz/30 g) pumpkin seeds

½ cup (5½ oz/170 g) maple syrup

3 Tbsp ground cinnamon

1 Tbsp ground nutmeg

½ tsp kosher salt

¼ cup (2 oz/60 g) firmly packed light brown sugar

¼ cup (3 oz/90 g) honey

Preheat the oven to 375°F (190°C). Spray two 9-by-13-inch (23-by-33-cm) rimmed baking sheets or one 18-by-13-inch (45-by-33-cm) rimmed baking sheet with nonstick cooking spray.

In a large bowl, toss together the oats, walnuts, almonds, sunflower seeds, pumpkin seeds, maple syrup, cinnamon, nutmeg, salt, and brown sugar. Spread the oat mixture evenly across the prepared baking sheets. Bake, stirring occasionally, until golden brown, about 25 minutes.

Remove from the oven and drizzle the granola evenly with the honey. Let cool on the baking sheets, then serve (or store in an airtight container at room temperature for up to 2 weeks).

sweet CLASSICS

dessert dishes that will always

IMPRESS & TASTE GREAT

Preserved Lemon Key Lime Pie 140 • Fernet Poached Pears 143

Chocolate Mousse with Hazelnut Streusel 144

Chocolate Cake with Strawberry Lava 145

Carrot Cake 148 • Apple Granola Crisp 149 • Bananas Foster 151

preserved lemon
KEY LIME PIE

This recipe, with its 7UP lemon-lime–inspired twist, is Eli's favorite pie dessert. There's something so quintessentially dineresque about it that reminds him of the 1950s. That's his favorite decade because he loves the idea of being a greaser from the wrong side of the tracks and taking the head cheerleader out for burgers and milk shakes while everyone else in the diner looks on disapprovingly. Rebel with a cause. And that cause is eating pie.

2 cups (6 oz/185 g) graham cracker crumbs

½ cup (4 oz/125 g) granulated sugar

4 Tbsp (2 oz/60 g) unsalted butter, melted and cooled

2 cans (14 oz/440 g each) sweetened condensed milk

2 large egg yolks

1 cup (8 fl oz/250 ml) Key lime or regular lime juice

1 cup (8 oz/250 g) crème fraîche

2 Tbsp finely diced preserved lemon

1 cup (8 fl oz/250 ml) heavy cream

1 lemon, for zesting

2 Tbsp confectioners' sugar

Preheat the oven to 375°F (190°C).

In a bowl, stir together the cracker crumbs, granulated sugar, and butter. Press the mixture firmly onto the bottom and up the sides of a 9-inch (23-cm) pie pan. Bake until browned, about 20 minutes. Transfer to a wire rack and let cool to room temperature.

Reduce the oven temperature to 325°F (165°C).

In a large bowl, whisk together the condensed milk and egg yolks until well blended. Add the lime juice and mix well, then fold in the crème fraîche and preserved lemon. Pour the filling into the cooled pie shell. Bake until the filling is set like a custard, about 15 minutes. Transfer to a wire rack to cool, then refrigerate, uncovered, for at least 4 hours or up to overnight.

When ready to serve, place a metal bowl in the freezer for 10 minutes. Remove the bowl, pour in the cream, and whisk until soft peaks form.

To serve, cut the pie into slices, transfer to individual plates, and top each slice with a dollop of the whipped cream. Grate a little lemon zest on each slice, then finish with a sprinkle of confectioners' sugar.

FERNET
poached pears

If you are used to poached pears that are sickly sweet, you've had them the wrong way at your grandma's house. Now have them the right way. The bitterness of the fernet, an herbaceous and aromatic spirit, is a perfect foil to the sweetness of the pears. If you are terrified of baking or need to focus your time on the main course, this fast and easy dessert is a conclusion to a meal that no one will forget.

2 cups (16 fl oz/500 ml) fernet

1 star anise pod

1 vanilla bean

1 cinnamon stick

4 ripe pears such as Bosc or Comice, peeled

4 Tbsp (1½ oz/45 g) chopped crystallized ginger

In a saucepan just large enough to fit the pears, combine the fernet, 1 cup (8 fl oz/ 250 ml) water, the star anise, vanilla bean, and cinnamon stick and bring to a simmer over medium-low heat.

Carefully place the pears in the simmering liquid and poach until tender, 10–15 minutes. Using a slotted spoon, transfer the pears to individual bowls.

Simmer the poaching liquid until it has reduced by half and has thickened, about 10 minutes. Remove and discard the star anise, vanilla bean, and cinnamon stick.

Drizzle the pears with the reduced liquid and top each serving with 1 tablespoon of the ginger. Serve right away.

CHOCOLATE MOUSSE
with hazelnut streusel

Ever since we saw Robin Leach eating chocolate mousse in a twenty-foot-long, diamond-encrusted bathtub, mousse has represented the epitome of luxury in our home. Winter's-day cold, light-as-air chocolate in a Champagne glass? Only the rich and famous would have access to such a sumptuous dessert option! Little did we know that chocolate mousse is just about the easiest dessert you can make. Here's a foolproof recipe to bring those Champagne riches and caviar dreams right into your own home (and bathtub).

1¼ cups (10 fl oz/310 ml) heavy cream

4 large egg whites

1 cup (4 oz/125 g) confectioners' sugar, plus more for dusting

6 oz (185 g) semisweet (65% cacao) chocolate

1 tsp almond extract

1 tsp pure vanilla extract

hazelnut streusel

1 cup (5 oz/155 g) all-purpose flour

½ cup (4 oz/125 g) granulated sugar

½ cup (4 oz/125 g) unsalted butter, cut into ½-inch (12-mm) pieces

½ cup (2 oz/60 g) chopped hazelnuts or a mixture of walnuts, hazelnuts, and almonds

Place 2 large metal bowls in the freezer for 10 minutes. Remove 1 bowl, pour in the cream, and whisk until stiff peaks form.

In the second bowl, whisk the egg whites until peaks begin to form. Gradually pour in the confectioners' sugar and continue to beat until large peaks form.

In the top pan of a double boiler, melt the chocolate over (but not touching) simmering water, stirring occasionally until smooth. Remove from the heat and let cool for 2 minutes. Pour the chocolate into the whipped cream and fold in gently with a spatula. Add the egg white mixture and the almond and vanilla extracts and fold in gently just until combined.

Spoon the mousse into 4–6 individual bowls, dividing evenly. Refrigerate, uncovered, for at least 1 hour before serving. Once the mousse is completely cool, it will keep, covered, in the refrigerator for up to 3 days.

To make the streusel, preheat the oven to 350°F (180°C). Line a baking sheet with parchment paper or a nonstick baking mat.

In a food processor, combine the flour and granulated sugar and pulse briefly to mix. Scatter the butter pieces evenly over the flour mixture, then pulse three times. Add the nuts and pulse briefly. The mixture should be crumbly. Spread it on the prepared baking sheet.

Bake until lightly browned, about 15 minutes. Let cool completely before using.

To serve, sprinkle each mousse with some of the streusel and dust with confectioners' sugar.

CHOCOLATE CAKE
with strawberry lava

We were young kids in 1997 when Hollywood brought us two of the finest volcano films ever, both of which revitalized the stale volcano-film genre. Tommy Lee Jones delivered a heartbreaking performance in *Volcano*, and Pierce Brosnan plucked our heartstrings as a volcanologist in *Dante's Peak*. We've seen them both hundreds, if not thousands, of times. And using those two classic films as inspiration, we've taken the molten lava cake of our youth and reinvented it as an actual volcano cake that erupts strawberry ganache when you slice it.

cake & ganache

2 Tbsp unsalted butter, melted and cooled to room temperature

9 oz (280 g) bittersweet chocolate, chopped

1 cup (8 oz/250 g) granulated sugar

¾ cup (6 fl oz/180 ml) canola oil

1 large egg

2 cups (10 oz/315 g) all-purpose flour

½ cup (1½ oz/45 g) unsweetened cocoa powder

1 Tbsp baking soda

¼ tsp kosher salt

1 cup (8 fl oz/250 ml) buttermilk

1 tsp pure vanilla extract

¼ cup (1 oz/30 g) confectioners' sugar

½ cup (4 fl oz/125 ml) heavy cream

lava

8 oz (250 g) white melting chocolate

1 cup (4 oz/125 g) strawberries, stemmed and chopped

1 tsp rose water

Pinch of kosher salt

To make the cake, place a rack in the lower third of the oven and preheat to 350°F (180°C). Using your hand or a paper towel, rub the butter thoroughly over all of the interior surfaces of a 10-inch (25-cm) Bundt pan, then spray with nonstick cooking spray.

In the top pan of a double boiler, melt 3 oz (90 g) of the chocolate over (but not touching) simmering water, stirring occasionally until smooth. Scrape the chocolate into a large bowl and whisk in the granulated sugar. Add the canola oil and whisk until smooth and fully incorporated. Add the egg and whisk until smooth.

In another bowl, whisk together the flour, cocoa powder, baking soda, and salt.

Add half of the flour mixture to the chocolate mixture and stir until fully incorporated. Add half of the buttermilk and whisk until incorporated. Repeat this process with the remaining flour mixture and buttermilk. Add the vanilla and mix well.

Pour the batter into the prepared pan. Bake until a toothpick inserted into the center of the cake comes out mostly clean (a few small crumbs are okay, but there should be no batter on the toothpick), about 45 minutes.

Let cool in the pan on a wire rack for 15 minutes. Invert a plate over the pan, invert the pan and plate together, and lift off the pan. Let the cake cool completely.

While the cake is cooling, make the ganache. In the top pan of a double boiler, melt the remaining 6 oz (185 g) chocolate over (but not touching) simmering water, stirring occasionally until smooth. Add the confectioners' sugar and stir well so it melts into the chocolate. Add ¼ cup (2 fl oz/60 ml) of the cream and stir well until smooth, then add the remaining ¼ cup (2 fl oz/60 ml) cream and stir well. Remove from the heat and let the ganache cool for a few minutes. It should be thick but pourable. Pour the ganache over the top of the cooled cake and let it set and harden for 30–45 minutes.

To make the lava, in the top pan of a double boiler, melt the white chocolate over (but not touching) simmering water, stirring occasionally until smooth. Fold in the strawberries and stir well. Add the rose water and salt and stir well. Once the mixture is smooth and pourable, pour it into the center of the cake. Cut into slices—the strawberry-laced lava will erupt as you cut—and serve.

CARROT CAKE

The plating of this dessert is like a choose-your-own adventure. You could go 1980s white-tablecloth, fine-dining style and serve a perfect square of cake topped with a quenelle of *semifreddo*. Or you could go hypermodern, tasting-menu style and arrange hunks of cake and rough jabs of *semifreddo* in a wide swath across the plate of "organized chaos." Whichever way you do it, you get to eat carrot cake, crème anglaise, and cream cheese *semifreddo*, so sometimes presentation just doesn't matter.

semifreddo

³/₄ lb (375 g) cream cheese, at room temperature

1 Tbsp ground cinnamon

5 cups (40 fl oz/1.25 l) heavy cream

1¹/₂ cups (12 oz/375 g) sugar

12 large eggs yolks

1 tsp almond extract

1 tsp pure vanilla extract

cake

4 large eggs

1¹/₄ cups (10 fl oz/310 ml) vegetable oil

1 tsp pure vanilla extract

2 cups (10 oz/315 g) all-purpose flour

2 cups (1 lb/500 g) sugar

2 tsp baking soda

2 tsp baking powder

¹/₂ tsp kosher salt

1 Tbsp ground cinnamon

1 tsp ground allspice

1 tsp ground cloves

¹/₂ tsp ground nutmeg

2 cups (10 oz/315 g) grated peeled carrots

crème anglaise

2 cups (16 fl oz/500 ml) heavy cream

¹/₂ cup (4 fl oz/125 ml) carrot juice

5 large egg yolks

¹/₂ cup (4 oz/125 g) sugar

1 cup (4 oz/125 g) pecans, toasted (optional)

To make the semifreddo, using a stand mixer fitted with the paddle attachment, beat together the cream cheese and cinnamon until smooth.

In a bowl, whisk the cream until soft peaks form. Add ½ cup (4 oz/125 g) of the sugar and whisk until stiff peaks form. Set aside.

In a large bowl, whisk together the egg yolks and the remaining 1 cup (8 oz/250 g) sugar until the mixture triples in volume. Add the almond and vanilla extracts and whisk to incorporate. Fold the egg yolk mixture into the whipped cream.

With the stand mixer on its lowest setting, gently fold in one-third of the yolk-cream mixture and beat until incorporated, 10–15 seconds. Remove the bowl from the mixer and, using a rubber spatula, fold in the remaining yolk-cream mixture. Pour into a 9-by-13-inch (23-by-33-cm) glass baking dish, cover with plastic wrap, and freeze overnight.

To make the cake, preheat the oven to 350°F (180°C). Line the bottom and sides of a 9-by-13-inch (23-by-33-cm) cake pan with parchment paper and grease the parchment.

In a large bowl, stir together the eggs, oil, vanilla, flour, sugar, baking soda, baking powder, salt, cinnamon, allspice, cloves, and nutmeg until well incorporated. Fold in the carrots.

Pour the batter into the prepared pan. Bake until a toothpick inserted into the center of the cake comes out clean, about 40 minutes. Let cool in the pan on a wire rack for 20 minutes. Invert a plate over the pan, invert the pan and plate together, and lift off the pan. Let cool completely.

Meanwhile, make the crème anglaise. In a saucepan, bring the cream and carrot juice to a simmer over high heat, then remove from the heat.

In a bowl, whisk the egg yolks and sugar until thick and frothy. Remove the cream sauce from the heat. Temper the egg yolks by adding 1 tablespoon of the cream sauce to the yolks and stirring gently. Continue adding the sauce, 1 tablespoon at a time, stirring well after each addition, until you have added ½ cup (4 fl oz/125 ml). Add the egg yolk mixture to the pan with the remaining sauce and stir gently until blended.

Place the pan over low heat and cook, stirring constantly to prevent the eggs from scorching and scrambling, until the custard has thickened and the back of a spoon leaves a trail when pulled gently through the mixture, 1–2 minutes. Remove from the heat and strain through a fine-mesh sieve into a bowl. Let cool, uncovered.

To serve, cut the cake into large pieces. Place a few spoonfuls of the crème anglaise on the bottom of each individual bowl, place a piece of cake in the center, and top with a scoop of the semifreddo. Sprinkle with the pecans, if desired.

apple granola
CRISP

Our mom makes a dynamite apple crisp. This recipe features the granola on page 137, so if you're reading this and you've already made the granola, good news, as dessert is only a few short steps away. And if you haven't made the granola yet, take control of your life. You should be eating more granola. Sit up straight. Listen to your doctor. Read a book. Seriously, get it together.

10 Granny Smith apples, peeled, cored, and cut into 1-inch (2.5-cm) pieces

1 cup (8 oz/250 g) granulated sugar

1 Tbsp all-purpose flour

½ recipe Cinnamon–Sunflower Seed Granola (page 137)

2 cups (16 fl oz/500 ml) heavy cream

2 Tbsp confectioners' sugar

1 Tbsp ground cinnamon

Preheat the oven to 350°F (180°C). Generously spray a 9-by-13-inch (23-by-33-cm) baking dish with nonstick cooking spray.

In a bowl, stir together the apples, granulated sugar, and flour. Pour into the prepared baking dish. Sprinkle the granola evenly on top. Cover with aluminum foil and bake for 25 minutes. Uncover and bake for an additional 10 minutes. The crisp should be golden brown around the edges and bubbling.

Meanwhile, place a metal bowl in the freezer for 10 minutes. Remove the bowl, pour in the cream, and whisk until soft peaks begin to form. Sprinkle in the confectioners' sugar and cinnamon and whisk well for 20 seconds to incorporate. Place the bowl in the refrigerator until ready to serve.

Using a large spoon, scoop the crisp into individual bowls and top each serving with a large dollop of the cinnamon whipped cream.

bananas FOSTER

In a land before time, our ancestors (monkey people) lived a peaceful existence, catching rays, taking naps, and picking bananas off trees. One night there was a terrible storm, and a bolt of lightning lit a banana tree on fire. Although most of the monkey people were scared, one approached the tree and picked off a banana that was still smoldering from the fire. He peeled it to find it was roasted and filled with delicious and complex flavors from the Maillard reactions of caramelization. It was unlike any other banana that had come before. And that's how we invented fire.

2 Tbsp unsalted butter

2 Tbsp firmly packed light brown sugar

¼ tsp kosher salt

2 bananas, peeled and halved lengthwise

¼ cup (2 fl oz/60 ml) dark rum

½ tsp pure vanilla extract

2 scoops vanilla or banana ice cream

In a wide sauté pan, melt the butter over medium heat. Add the sugar and salt and stir just until the sugar dissolves. Add the bananas and cook, turning once, until golden brown on both sides, about 1 minute on each side.

Remove the pan from the heat and add the rum and vanilla. Very carefully return the pan to medium heat and use a long stick lighter to ignite the rum. Cook for 30 seconds so the alcohol burns off, then remove from the heat.

Put a scoop of ice cream on each individual plate. Divide the bananas between the plates and spoon the pan sauce over the top. Serve right away.

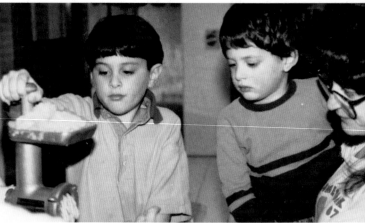

INDEX

To Papa, we wouldn't be anywhere without your having led us by example. We miss you very much.

To our Nana and our aunts and uncles—Ronnie, Lonnie, Beth, Sandy Marshall, Eve, and Hardy—for loving and supporting everything we've ever done.

THANKS

Our parents thanks for the inspiration and for continuing to let us exploit our childhood for food credibility, cute pictures, and cookbook sales. We will soon stop making fun of you publicly.

Kate the excitement doesn't end! There's no one I would rather share a plum with.

Amy thank you for chasing us down via email phone text and page to get this book done. You would make a great private detective! We are thankful we have your eyes on our project to make it successful.

Ali and the art team as usual, your instincts and vision win out to produce both a cookbook that looks good and works really well. Thanks for dealing with our oft-conflicting versions of what we thought this book was supposed to be; it turned out for the better!

Erin and Shay lets make this a yearly thing right? You come to NYC, we try not to poison you with chicken delivery from some average restaurant, and you take the best pictures of food the world has ever seen. Not a bad thing to look forward to right?

Simon and Hadas it has taken us a few years, but we now realize being a food stylist means doing most of the actual work that goes into publishing a cookbook! You do a beautiful job and we love cooking with you in the kitchen. Simon, next time you go on some kayaking/biking/fishing adventure please take us with you. Your life looks much better than ours.

Paige and Jenna You have the finest collection of old-timey plates and platters on the Eastern seaboard!

You really helped make this book something special. We hope one day you can prop style our apartments.

Recipe testers thanks for your feedback and for spending your time to help make our recipes better and easier to comprehend, thank you thank you thank you. This book wouldn't exist without a little help from our friends.

Adrienne and Columbia Products who knew that the perfect food photo studio not only existed but that it was right off the Montrose stop? You guys were such great hosts that we want to write another cookbook just to spend a week at your place.

Noah thanks for another great year at the restaurants, and another great cookbook that you've supported from the beginning. Thank you for the opportunity to run your restaurants. It's not a job I take lightly and I strive every day to make them better. You are a great friend and an even better restaurateur mentor.

Max Aronson you are the champagne in my champagne bubble bath.

Colin you are the wind beneath my wings in the song you are the wind beneath my wings.

The Fat Jew how can one man be so unbelievably talented and attractive while also being a doctor and a lawyer and saving children from starvation and puppies from being abandoned? We cannot wait to donate to your campaign for president. You are going to mop the floor with Chelsea Clinton.

Olive Press

Recipes and text © Copyright 2014
Eli Sussman and Max Sussman

Images and illustrations © Copyright 2014
Weldon Owen, Inc.

Olive Press is an imprint of
Weldon Owen, Inc. and Williams-Sonoma, Inc.

www.weldonowen.com

www.williams-sonoma.com

Weldon Owen, Inc. is a division of **BONNIER**
1045 Sansome Street, Suite 100
San Francisco, CA 94111

Library of Congress Control Number:
2014959876

ISBN 13: 978-1-61628-812-9
ISBN 10: 1-61628-812-4

Printed and bound in China
by Toppan-Leefung Printers Limited

First printed in 2014
10 9 8 7 6 5 4 3 2 1